THE GIF

The Gifts
of the Spirit

CECIL COUSEN

KINGSWAY PUBLICATIONS
EASTBOURNE

ISBN 0 86065 477 X

Biblical quotations are from the
Authorized Version (crown copyright)

Front cover design by Vic Mitchell

Printed in Great Britain for
KINGSWAY PUBLICATIONS LTD
Lottbridge Drove, Eastbourne, E. Sussex BN23 6NT by
Cox & Wyman Ltd, Reading.
Typeset by CST, Eastbourne, E. Sussex.

Contents

Foreword

I am delighted to write this foreword, to introduce not only the book, but its author, who has been a personal friend for over twenty years. In the 1960s the emerging renewal movement in Britain owed a lot to four men, who influenced it significantly. Edgar Trout taught us about spiritual warfare; Arthur Wallis showed us how to teach from the Bible; Campbell McAlpine taught us about personal holiness; and Cecil Cousen majored on *faith*. In the early days of the Fountain Trust all four figured prominently, and both Arthur Wallis and Cecil Cousen spoke at the famous Guildford Conference in 1971.

Circumstances have removed these men from their former influence. Edgar Trout died, Campbell McAlpine left for the United States (though it is good to know that he is back again in Britain), Arthur Wallis became increasingly involved in the growing Restoration Movement, and concentrated largely in that field, and Cecil Cousen has been somewhat restricted in his ministry through the illness of his wife Jean. It is, therefore, all the more important that we are now able to have Cecil's teaching in book form.

Cecil is no theologian, and he has never claimed to be that. But he has always been a brilliant communicator, and when you read this book you will realize how a whole generation of us benefited from his balanced and eminently sensible teaching. The Lord gave us Cecil at a time when we were all new to charismatic gifts. Much of the success of the transplanting process that took place is due to Cecil.

There was one particularly important phase in the life of Cecil Cousen which influenced him profoundly. He witnessed the famous 'Latter Rain' revival in Canada. Unlike most of us he has experienced revival, seen the depth and height. The real thing always spoils us for anything else. But some of the revival went wrong. Cecil experienced that too, and this no doubt injected an important cautionary element into his approach. He knew what was real and what was counterfeit, he knew what was deep and what was mere froth.

You will not agree with everything in this book, but you will enjoy its sweet spirit of reasonableness. Cecil is Anglican at this point. I hope that its appeal will not only be to my generation, which respected these elder statesmen, but to the important new generation of Christians, which shows such promise. If they follow the principles in this book they will not go far wrong. I particularly commend Cecil's teaching on interpretation of tongues. I have never seen it put better.

In the sixties there were virtually no charismatic magazines (until *Renewal* came on the scene in 1966). But Cecil was producing one called *A Voice of Faith*, and it was compulsive reading, even at the breakfast table when it arrived. Some of my old copies have marmalade stains on them to this day! It was typical of

Cecil's innate modesty that he insisted on calling it *A* rather than *The Voice of Faith*. He never allowed himself to be made a spiritual guru, and he never claimed infallibility. He was a voice crying in the desert, and his main message was always *faith*. The chapters on this subject in this book are particularly inspiring. But then Cecil always was inspiring when he got going on his pet subject. I will never forget some of those talks, and one of his favourite phrases, 'when God does it, it's easy'.

The Lord took Cecil through a dark tunnel when Jean was suddenly taken seriously ill. How the devil loves to taunt apostles of faith when their loved ones are suffering! Cecil wrestles honestly with this in his book. It reminds one of another classic, *Nine O'clock in the Morning*, when Dennis Bennett recounts his first wife's death from cancer. But the Lord saved the life of Jean, and Cecil lovingly nursed and cared for her until they were able to travel together again. Cecil never budged in the face of this trial, and came through it—as he has inspired all of us to do—'by faith'.

I hope that this book will be widely read. We need this sort of teaching as a new generation emerges. Cecil is a man of compassion and conviction. That has been the secret of his life. It meant that he commended himself to all kinds of Christians. He is as much at home in an Anglican church as in a Pentecostal one. In writing this foreword I salute a man of God who has contributed greatly to my own understanding of the Holy Spirit, and I'm sure his ministry will continue to inspire many.

MICHAEL HARPER

A Word of Explanation

Two points need a word of explanation.

First: I have deliberately put the chapter on 'tongues' before the other gifts, not to suggest it has any prior importance, neither because of its being first in controversy, but only because it illustrates so well the point of the 'partnership of the Spirit', which I consider to be an important basis for the working of all the gifts of the Spirit.

Second: I have used the Authorized Version throughout. I have lived a lifetime in fellowship with the AV and cannot get used to using many modern translations good (and bad!) as some of them are. I tried very hard for a couple of years to turn over to the Revised Standard Version when it first came out, but without success.

One cannot easily change a lifetime's thought patterns. That is not to say I do not appreciate the best of the new translations: I refer to them regularly. But more importantly, what I do all the time is to check the Hebrew and Greek in Young's Concordance, not only for the original meaning but also for all the other

English words by which any Hebrew or Greek word is translated elsewhere in the Scriptures, and also for the *contexts* of these other references.

Finally I quote Dr Martyn Lloyd-Jones on the subject. Referring to Acts 19:2 in *Joy Unspeakable* (Kingsway, 1984, page 31) he writes: 'from a purely linguistic standpoint the Authorized Version translation is wrong, but, as so often, these Authorized translators get the right point, the right meaning, but they over-emphasize it a little. . . .'

These early translators really believed what they were translating, they were prepared to be burned at the stake for it; and they had no intention of 'watering it down' to accommodate any modern unbelieving theology or neo-psychological views of the nature of man.

I

Two Streams

The last great day of the feast was a day of great joy, loud jubilation and the sounding of trumpets. The priest went in solemn procession from the pool of Siloam, bearing in a golden vessel water which he poured out from the top of the temple steps in the sight of the assembled crowd of people. They were quite likely chanting 'With joy shall ye draw water out of the wells of salvation' (Is 12:3).

It was immediately after this ceremony that Jesus stood in some prominent place and cried: 'If any man thirst, let him come unto me, and drink' (Jn 7:37). The water of which Jesus spoke, adds John, is the Holy Spirit—the same water that Jesus told the woman at the well would be 'in [her] a well of water springing up into everlasting life' (Jn 4:14).

Two streams

This giving of the water of life is the first stream of the Holy Spirit's ministry: the stream of life and life-giving.

It is at the heart of the Good News; it is prominent throughout the New Testament, and still there are the final verses of John's Revelation, 'I will give unto him that is athirst of the fountain of the water of life freely' and, 'let him that is athirst come. And whosoever will, let him take the water of life freely' (Rev 21:6; 22:17).

There is a second stream. Quite unexpectedly, almost illogically, Jesus on the feast day went on to say, 'He that believeth on me, as the scripture hath said, out of his belly shall flow rivers of living water.'

In the first stream, as one drinks, the water goes *in;* in the second stream it comes *out.*

The word translated 'belly' in the AV is rendered 'womb' twelve times in the NT (AV). This may hold significant implications because the second stream of water flowing out refers to the Spirit's ministry of power, the operation of spiritual gifts in their widest interpretation. And these need to issue from a spiritual womb, the place, deep within human personality, where the already resident Spirit conceives and brings to birth spiritual ministry. Only from such a source is ministry authentic and effective in the kingdom of heaven on earth. There is only one Holy Spirit, but he has this two-fold ministry. The first is fundamental and well understood. It is to the second we shall direct our attention.

Until recently most teaching and writing about the Holy Spirit has concerned his person, his life-giving and sanctifying ministry—the first stream—and related mainly to the teaching of John chapters 14–16. The Holy Spirit of the Acts of the Apostles, the same person portrayed in action, chiefly relates to the second stream.

It is important to bring together the passages in John's gospel and the Acts of the Apostles and as we do so to consider the word 'comforter' used in John's gospel. It is the same word translated 'advocate' in 1 John 2:1, a well-known verse which speaks of Jesus being our advocate with the Father. Jesus is our advocate in heaven. Whose advocate is the Holy Spirit? He is Christ's advocate on earth. An advocate is one who speaks and acts for another. The Holy Spirit does just that for the exalted Christ.

Jesus promised to send 'another Advocate', using the Greek word meaning 'another *of the same kind*', which explains how he could also say, 'I will not leave you comfortless: I will come to you.' We are quite familiar with the idea of Christ being our advocate in heaven and we go to him regularly for his cleansing and help. The Holy Spirit in his advocate ministry on earth is amongst us to speak and act for our Lord, who is the same yesterday, today and for ever . . . Which leads me to the opening words of the book of Acts where Luke refers to his gospel, the earlier record 'of all that Jesus began both to do and teach'. This phrase is the key to the understanding of the whole of the book of Acts; it brings together the teaching of John's gospel and the Acts of the Apostles. In the simplicity of the little phrase two things are fundamental:

1) That Jesus (only) began.
2) He began to do and teach. Both.

The first underlines the fact that Jesus during his time on earth only began his ministry, implying that it was to continue, which is what this book sets out to tell, and which unlike most of the books of the New Testament, finishes without any 'Amen' at the end, with the further implication that it is still to continue.

The second underlines that Jesus, now as then, is doing as well as teaching. The combination of the word of God and action by the Holy Spirit is basic in God's economy. In the beginning God said, 'Let there be light' and immediately the Holy Spirit 'moved' upon the face of the waters. The Latin word used for 'moved' is *incubabat,* from which we get our English word 'incubate'. Again, when God was sending his Son to be incarnate among men, he sent his word to Mary and immediately promised that the Holy Spirit would 'come upon' her and the 'power of the Highest overshadow' her. In the same vein, the gospel of Mark concludes: 'And they went forth . . . the Lord working with them, and confirming the word with signs following.' In the Greek the word 'them' is not actually present, which means that the passage could read: 'The Lord working with, and confirming the word . . .' The Lord always does 'work with' his word, and the result is what we call 'signs and wonders'.

All this was normal in the early church, as Conybeare writes: 'The feature which most immediately forces itself upon our notice, as distinctive of the church in the apostolic age is its possession of supernatural gifts . . . the exercise of such gifts is spoken of as a matter of ordinary occurrence.' The modern church, by contrast, has concentrated on 'word' almost to the exclusion of action. We have been like the church at Ephesus before the arrival of St Paul. Apollos was a brilliant preacher, a learned man, mighty in the Scriptures and 'fervent in spirit'. Literally he 'boiled over in spirit' i.e. he was really enthusiastic. Samuel Chadwick remarks that enthusiasm does not often accompany scholarship. It is bad form amongst cultured people.

Today we have plenty of scholarship but few who are 'mighty in the Scriptures' and possibly fewer who have any enthusiasm for spiritual things. These human abilities, splendid as they are in their proper setting, are useless to build the church which is the body of Christ.

Chadwick writes again: 'To run an organisation needs no God. Men can supply energy, enterprise and enthusiasm for things human. The real work of the church depends upon the power of the Spirit.'

It was because Jesus foresaw this human tendency and the total inadequacy of human words and methods that he insisted that his disciples should 'tarry' until they were 'endued with power from on high'. Later Jesus equated this command to being 'baptized with the Holy Spirit', which again he later defined as 'the Holy Spirit coming upon you'; which in turn, of course, was fulfilled on the day of Pentecost. All this holds both pattern and meaning for the whole church age.

Because of this instruction of Jesus, it became normal practice amongst the early Pentecostals to hold what they called 'tarrying meetings' for those seeking to be baptized in the Spirit. That was fair enough; and God answered their faith. He still does, and always will. But in the so-called charismatic movement we have been shown by the Spirit that there is no need to 'tarry' but rather to receive now. (More of this later.) Tarry or not, the assumption has been that to be baptized in the Spirit is to receive power. This ought to be true, but unfortunately in most cases it is not.

To illustrate, using the same metaphor of water, if I bring my vessel (myself) to be filled with water and if the glass is already 7/8th full of stones or other rubbish, then even Almighty God can only fill 1/8th of the glass with water. It is of his grace that he will do just that, and he does. We then say that a person is baptized with the Holy Spirit, is filled with the Spirit . . .

But sadly, usually, not much 'power from on high' is evident. So maybe it is time for us to return to the practice of 'tarrying' not for the baptism, but, as Jesus originally said, for 'power from on high'. This power brings a dimension of spiritual life and ministry where the gifts of the Spirit, viewed in their largest context, are the normal tools for the job, for the individual to live effectively in the good of the kingdom and for the church, the body of Christ, to fulfil its purpose as a body, namely to be a means of location and expression for the personality indwelling it.

Power from on high in the NT is always spoken of with the use of the preposition 'upon'. It comes from above and so naturally falls 'upon'. This has to do with the Spirit at work. His life-giving ministry is always referred to with the preposition 'in' or 'within'.

We shall follow our theme largely under these two headings: 'within' and 'upon'.

These two streams of the Spirit's ministry obviously overlap, and so before proceeding to our main theme of 'upon'; we shall pause to consider briefly the 'within' aspect.

2

The Holy Spirit 'Within'

Jesus introduces this thought by first using the preposition 'with' in John 14:17: '. . . he dwelleth with you, and shall be in you'. It is good to have the Spirit with us; it is this which causes people to be aware of God's presence in a church building. This is the 'sweet influence' of the traditional hymn. It generates an atmosphere of reverence.

We may surely claim that the Holy Spirit has been with us as a nation over the last two centuries; it has made us, for all our faults and satanic mills, a Christian country. It caused our people to base its legal structure on the ten commandments, to respect the Lord's day and to attend, at least occasionally, the Lord's house. There is a strange passage in Paul's second letter to the Thessalonians: 'For the mystery of lawlessness is already at work; only he who now restrains it will do so until he is out of the way' (2 Thess 2:7 RSV). This is generally understood to refer to the Holy Spirit's restraining influence. It would be a bold assertion to say that he is already taken 'out of the way' in our country;

19

but sadly, it almost appears that he has begun his departure. Certainly less and less of each new generation seem to be aware that the Holy Spirit is with them.

All who seek the presence of God will find that the Holy Spirit will come to be 'with' them. May their number increase! But that would only give us more and more 'nominal Christians'.

It is the 'within-ness' that is the *sine qua non* of real Christians. Paul says, 'Now if any man have not the Spirit of Christ, he is none of his' (Rom 8:9). And John is even more insistent, '. . . God hath given to us eternal life, and this life is in his Son. He that hath the Son hath (this) life; and he that hath not the Son of God hath not life' (1 Jn 5:11–12).

The 'within-ness' of the Spirit is the 'new' of the New Testament. It was promised by Jeremiah and Ezekiel and confirmed by our Lord: '[He] shall be in you. . . I will not leave you comfortless: I will come to you. . . because I live ye shall live also' (Jn 14:17–19). It is Christ 'in us' that is the new creation for any man that is 'in Christ' (strange but glorious Christian terminology!).

It is sad that so many very sincere and godly folk who frequent our churches never get further than the experience of forgiveness. That is wonderful and basic, of course, but it should be regarded as clearing away the rubbish that precludes a person from getting through the door into new life.

I remember leading a communion service where Michael Harper was the preacher. He started his sermon by saying that Jesus did not die on the cross to forgive us our sins! He put it like that for effect, of course, and went on to say that the purpose of forgiveness is that we may receive new life. But he caused some lifted eyebrows for a moment.

Paul put it like this: 'For if, when we were enemies,

20

we were reconciled to God by the death of his Son, much more, being reconciled, we shall be saved by his life' (Rom 5:10). We are saved by his life firstly as our high priest at the throne of grace, but also as our indwelling life. 'I am the . . . life', said Jesus. Notice 'I am'; not 'I have'.

Paul also speaks of the 'inner man' and the 'new man', and the climax of his second prayer in Ephesians is: 'That Christ may dwell in your hearts by faith . . . that ye may be filled with all the fulness of God . . . according to the power that worketh in us' (Eph 3:17–20). To have the Spirit 'with' us is good. To have the Spirit 'upon' us will be the main concern of this book; but to have the Spirit 'within' is fundamental and all-important.

What a salvation is this, what manner of men ought we to be, for 'in Christ dwelleth all the fulness of the Godhead bodily'? To think that we may possess him; he is ours, he is our life! This is life indeed, more abundant and eternal. This was the ultimate purpose of Calvary. Herein is regal sonship: 'Beloved, now we are the sons of God'. Jesus' purpose was 'to bring many sons to glory'.

Forgiveness is important; wonderful and essential, but preparatory. Worship is important but without life is unacceptable to God. The heart of a man without a new creation (Christ's Spirit within) is deceitful and desperately wicked; and the 'thoughts of the wicked are an abomination to the Lord' (Prov 15:26). 'In vain they do worship me' said Jesus to the Pharisees (Mt 15:9), and Amos—long before—had set the pace when he declared: 'I hate your show and pretence—your hypocrisy of "honouring" me with your religious feasts and solemn assemblies . . . Away with your hymns of praise—they are mere noise to my ears. I will not listen to your music, no matter how lovely it is' (Amos 5:21–23, The Living Bible). Healing is important but spiritual healing from death to life is more so. Doctrine is important too, but without life it is merely cerebral, what Paul calls 'the letter', and the letter kills, ministers death, even if the theology is correct.

It is out from the life *within* that the fruits of the Spirit grow, the expression of God's righteousness and character. Our subject is power and usefulness; but both are only possible on the basis of new life. Power is good; life is essential; but never does the New Testament speak of them as 'either/or'. 'Follow after charity, *and* desire spiritual gifts' is the constant emphasis (1 Cor 14:1).

Without holiness (from life within) no man shall see the Lord. Without power we may see him, but we shall be ashamed. Life is the 'gift of God', the first and most fundamental of the 'charismata'.

Every real Christian *has the Spirit*. Because there has been so much recrimination about this, it is important to get this foundation established right at the start.

Life is always 'within'. The preposition 'upon' is never used about life or regeneration. . . But the 'upon-ness' will be the subject of the rest of this book.

3

The Holy Spirit 'Upon'

The first stream of the Holy Spirit's ministry, as we have seen, is the giving and sustaining of new life, the gift of God. In order that this Good News can be efficiently and extensively preached and demonstrated, the second stream of power is important. In some aspects, essential; in all aspects important. This is the 'upon-ness' of the Spirit.

The question as to whether it is just important or essential hinges on the realization that regeneration itself is the major manifestation of power in the first place. A changed, victorious and sanctified Christian life is a major evidence of the power of the Spirit. If we accept this, as indeed we must, then the other manifestations of power are important but not absolutely essential in the furtherance of the gospel.

The gospel has been preached for centuries, and still is preached effectively with the only confirmation of the word being the testimony of changed lives. This is the evangelical message. Thank God for it; may it prosper and be enlarged in every way. The burden of this book is that this prosperity and growth can be so much more if there is the added content of the operation of the gifts of the Spirit in the outreach message.

I was invited some time ago to address a week's conference of evangelical missionaries in Morocco. One dear lady who had laboured there for thirty years invited me to her home for tea. After tea she asked me if I would like to see her church. Naturally I said yes, expecting to go down the street to some mission hall. Imagine my surprise, therefore, when she asked me to follow her through the kitchen into the back yard. There I was led into a little shed, not unlike a place to keep gardening tools, about the size of a terrace-house front room. Spotlessly clean, four bare walls and half a dozen cushions on the floor—and that was all after thirty years!

In the conference I was taking a consecutive Bible study from the book of Esther, and midway intended to introduce the 'charismatic' element—the coming-upon-ness of the Spirit, using Mordecai as a type of the Spirit. Knowing the nature of the conference I thought it only courtesy to mention this to the responsible leaders and ask their permission to proceed along these lines. I met two or three of them and to my surprise, they were considerably embarrassed at my intention; so I quickly suggested that maybe they would like to consult with their brethren and think and pray about it and let me know their decision later. They jumped at the idea. Later the leader came back to me, even more embarrassed with the answer: 'No.' They would prefer me not to proceed in that way. I hastily assured him I would respect their wishes.

So at the next session I switched to something entirely different without comment as to why. These people knew their Bibles well and knew that I had announced that I would take a full Bible study of Esther. I had only hinted at what was to follow in the next session; so they were puzzled at the sudden change and not a little intrigued but also not slow to surmise the likely reason. This made a greater impact, I am inclined to think, than if I had gone right on with my study.

The story had an ironic ending. Later in the week they had invited a Christian group from a nearby American army base to come and take one whole session. This they did with typical American verve—and charismatic witness! And further, they opened the session for public testimony, whereupon one of their own missionaries, recently baptized in the Spirit, stood and gave a glowing witness to this experience!

The next morning one of the missionaries, a delightful, sincere and godly man took an early morning devotional, speaking beautifully from Psalm 103: 'Bless the Lord, O my soul, and forget not all his benefits: who forgiveth all thine iniquities . . .' and there he abruptly stopped.

Afterwards I thanked him for an inspiring word and as politely as possible, with the thought of the lady-missionary's 'church' in mind, asked him why he had omitted to mention the rest of the verse, 'Who healeth all thy diseases'. I referred to the many poverty-stricken sick people of which there are so many in hot Third World countries, suggesting that a ministry of healing would very considerably enlarge the appeal and effectiveness of their proclamation of the Good News. But he would have none of it. Embarrassed, he just walked away.

We live in a sophisticated, technological world, and a multicultural, multireligious society (to say nothing of our diversified denominational variations) each with its own specific point of view. In the light of such variety the man in the street has every right to ask—and he does!—'How am I to know which religion or which denomination is right?' Generally he gets no satisfactory answer and so he writes church and religion off altogether.

There is only one effective answer to that legitimate query, the answer Jesus applied to himself and his ministry: 'If I do not *the works* of my Father, believe me not. But if I do, though ye believe not me, *believe the works*: that ye may know, and believe, that the Father is in me, and I in him' (Jn 10:37–8). The message which is confirmed 'with signs following' commands attention—and draws a crowd too! It was the message of the early Christians: Jesus, whom you crucified, is alive—and doing the same things as before.

The ministry of the gifts of the Spirit flow out from this second stream, the stream of power or enablement, the source of signs and wonders.

Jesus introduced this second stream with the words: 'He that believeth . . .' This he reiterated before he ascended: 'these signs shall follow *them that believe*'. Believing is always specific; one doesn't just believe, one believes for something definite. The passage therefore means: '. . . shall follow them that believe for signs and wonders'.

J. B. Phillips writing of this kind of believing in the Preface to *The Young Church in Action* (Geoffrey Bles, 1955)—which he calls the 'x-faculty'—has this to say:

Can we not see that it is the x-faculty which has deteriorated over the centuries . . . it has become atrophied almost to vanishing point. Now, since it is obvious throughout the New Testament that the x-faculty is the indispensable link between the resources of the unseen world and this temporary one, we can easily understand how the serious falling off in the use and practice of 'faith' throughout the church at large has resulted in a marked loss of spiritual power.

We shall revert to this subject in the chapter on the gift of faith; suffice it to insist at the moment that it is essential for a man of God to be 'full of faith and of the Holy Ghost' (Acts 6:5) if he is to do 'great wonders and miracles among the people' (6:8).

Our immediate concern is about being filled with the Spirit. Paradoxically, this phrase is always used in the NT to express the effect of the Holy Spirit coming 'upon' a person and never refers to a person possessing the life of the Spirit (i.e. the 'within-ness').

Luke records that the people of Samaria were already baptized in water in the name of the Lord Jesus, but that 'as yet [the Holy Spirit] was fallen *upon* none of them' (Acts 8:16). This condition was remedied by the ministry of Peter and John, who laid hands on them and they 'received the Holy Ghost'. It is patently obvious that to become regenerate is never effected by the laying on of hands.

The 'upon-ness' of the Spirit is not new to the New Testament, it is often found in the Old Testament; but before Pentecost it was only for special people for special occasions (see below). Since Pentecost it has been available to all who have the Spirit within as new life. Let us trace the meaning of 'upon-ness'.

The promise of the Father

Jesus had promised 'the Comforter, which is the Holy Ghost, whom the Father will send in my name' in the upper room discourse (Jn 14:26) and on resurrection morning he reaffirmed the promise: 'And behold, I send the promise of my Father *upon* you' (Lk 24:49). They were to wait for it, that is, 'until they were endued with power from on high'. The 'promise of the Father', the 'coming upon of the Spirit' is equated with 'power from on high'.

Why the promise of the Father? We can imagine in eternity the Father asks: 'Who will go to the sin-sick planet earth?' (see Is 59:16; 63:5). Jesus answered: 'I will go, but I ask that when I have finished the redeeming work of Calvary (ordained since before the foundation of the world) you will give the same Spirit of life and power to the redeemed ones that I will have had while on earth.'

Whether we are allowed to put human thinking and logic into the mind and mouth of deity is arguable; but at least it sheds some possible illumination on the phrase. To conclude the heavenly conversation, if we may, the Father agreed and promised. So when Jesus returned he received the fulfilment and Peter could say on the day of Pentecost: 'Therefore being by the right hand of God exalted, and having received of the Father the promise of the Holy Ghost, he hath shed forth this, which ye now see and hear' (Acts 2:33). The Spirit 'within' cannot be referred to intelligently as something which 'you now see and hear'. It refers to the upon-ness, to 'power from on high'.

This is the subject that Jesus spoke of immediately *after* his resurrection and again, immediately *before* his ascension. It must have been uppermost in his mind. On resurrection morning he equates the 'promise of the Father' with 'power from on high', and then on ascension day he equates them both to being 'baptized with the Holy Spirit', which in turn, he then goes on to define as 'You will receive the power of the Holy Spirit coming upon you'. This, of course, happened on the day of Pentecost.

In this final talk with his disciples Jesus parallels

being baptized with the Spirit to John's baptizing people with water. In every baptism there are three constituents: (1) the person being baptized; (2) the person doing the baptizing; and (3) the medium into which the person is to be baptized. So as Jesus relates John's baptizing to Pentecost the parallel is with item (3): in one case into water; in the other into the Holy Spirit. It is not sensible to speak of being baptized into a person. Although the theologians have used the phrase and made it sound familiar, being similar to being 'baptized unto Moses' (see 1 Cor 10:2), the preposition is not the same in the two cases, and the parallel is not sustainable.

Much less is it sensible to speak of one person falling upon another person. Hence Acts 1:8 is correctly translated: 'You will receive the power of the Holy Spirit coming upon you'. To try and get over this difficulty— and this objection to what I am sure is the true meaning —some translators have substituted 'to' for 'upon': i.e. 'coming to you'; but this is not correct. If we accept that 'upon' is always associated with 'power from on high' then there is no problem.

I have preached for many years that 'within' refers to regeneration and 'upon' always and only to empowering. But when I began research for this book I found that E. W. Bullinger in *The Giver and His Gifts* (The Lamp Press Ltd.) gives a long, detailed and learned treatment of the Greek in the matter, pointing out that there is a major difference between the use and non-use of the definite article in relation to the Holy Spirit i.e. between *the* Holy Spirit (and sometimes: *the* Holy *the* Spirit) and Holy Spirit. He insists that the former (with the article) always means the person of the Spirit and the latter (without the article) his gifts—his 'power from on high'.

To illustrate, in Acts 2:4 both forms are used: 'They were all filled with Holy Spirit (without the article, meaning his power) as *the* Holy Spirit (with the article, meaning the person) gave them utterance.'

The concept of Holy Spirit without the article is consistent with the idea of power as something into which one can be immersed. Admittedly, here again, we have become somewhat familiar with the idea of being immersed with the Holy Spirit (the person?) because of constant usage and the parallel with being baptized unto Moses.

Again, we can have much or little of the power from on high, a well accepted concept and certainly one true to experience, whereas one must have a whole person or none at all; one cannot have a bit of a person, especially if that person is the Holy Spirit. All of which underlines that for the Spirit to 'come upon' a person means it is power from on high that is coming upon him, which in turn is often related to being 'filled with the Spirit', a phrase never used in connection with the person of the Spirit being resident within a Christian. Rather, being 'filled with the Spirit' is nearly always followed by a reference to some consequent outflow or manifestation of the Spirit's power or ability. It was the ability to speak in tongues on the day of Pentecost, in Samaria and in the house of Cornelius; whereas in Ephesians (Eph 5:18–19) it is speaking to one another in psalms and hymns and spiritual songs. When Paul first arrived in Ephesus, the twelve disciples spoke with tongues *and* prophesied.

As mentioned above, on the day of Pentecost Peter referred to this infilling as something which could be 'seen and heard'. The person of the Spirit cannot be seen!

The Greek word for 'Spirit' is used by Paul in 1 Corinthians 14:12 and is translated in the AV by 'spiritual gifts' and in the RSV by 'manifestations of the Spirit'. Similarly, when introducing the whole subject of the *charismata* in 1 Corinthians 12:1 he makes an adjective into a noun, which is often (rightly) translated loosely into 'Now concerning *spirituals* I would not have you ignorant.' He then goes on to speak of spiritual gifts and/or the spiritual dimension, but certainly not of the person of the Spirit himself.

So to summarize: to be baptized with water by John in Jordan meant to be immersed into water, so to be baptized with the Spirit means to be immersed into the Spirit's power or enablement or into a spiritual dimension of living. This is when the 'promise of the Father' falls *upon* a person.

Later in this chapter we will look at the 'upon-ness' of the Spirit in the Old Testament, because it gives insight into the *purposes* of such an experience. Now let us see its use in the New Testament.

Mary

'The Spirit shall come upon thee' (Lk 1:35). This is immediately explained or augmented by 'the power of the Highest shall overshadow thee'. This power was manifested in the conception of the child Jesus; it was felt by Elizabeth, so much so that Elizabeth herself was filled with the Holy Spirit as a result of Mary just greeting her. This filling with the Holy Spirit caused Elizabeth to speak out 'with a loud voice', and virtually to prophesy, as Mary herself immediately went on to do in words that are still used, sacred and inspiring.

Jesus himself

'The Holy Spirit descended . . . "upon" him' (Lk 3:22). Jesus was conceived and born 'out from' the Holy

31

Spirit, and the very meaning of the incarnation is that God who is Spirit became resident in a human body. Uniquely and absolutely Jesus had the Holy Spirit 'within'; yet, even in his case, it is recorded that at Jordan the Spirit came 'upon' him.

The dove may well represent the person of the Spirit, but this doesn't alter the fact that before the 'coming upon' Jesus performed no miracle, preached no sermon, healed no sick people and no one knew who he was—except Mary who kept all these things hidden in her heart— whereas, after the 'coming upon' Luke records in correct translation: 'And Jesus, being about thirty years of age, began . . .'. Began what? The manifestation of the Spirit, or otherwise, his ministry.

All the rest of Luke 3 is taken up with his genealogy, a long list of names. The next verse of narrative (Lk 4:1) tells that Jesus was 'filled with the Spirit' (no article) i.e. with power from on high; and he was 'led by the Spirit' (with the article). The next sabbath he stands in his own local church and being asked to read the lesson, he 'found the place' in the Scriptures. In our Bible it was Isaiah 61:1. He knew what he was looking for, and he knew where to find it (preachers, take note!), and he read: 'The Spirit of the Lord is *upon* me . . .' and immediately identified its meaning and purpose: anointed to preach . . . to heal . . . to deliver . . . and to set at liberty.

Incidentally, to underline the point, it is obvious that 'anointing' is not an internal thing. Ointment is put on the body not into it. Similarly oil, which is a constant type of the Spirit, is always in the Bible applied externally, and never used as salad oil!

This passage is absolutely basic to the whole ministry of our Lord whilst on earth. His ministry was not in the power of his godhead, but always in the power of his anointed manhood. He retained his deity, of course, but ministered as an anointed man—his favourite name was the 'Son of man'. This raises vast and important issues which we cannot follow in detail here save to refer the reader to Philippians 2:6–8; John 5:19, 30; and John 14:10. This last verse leads on to verse 12 where Jesus promises that 'He that believeth on me, the works that I do shall he do also . . .' That is, this same anointing for power is available to us.

This whole subject is the background to Luke 24:49 where the disciples are told to tarry until they are endued with power from on high. Jesus was saying in effect, I didn't *begin* until the Spirit came *upon* me. See to it that you don't!

The citizens of Samaria

It is futile to suggest, as some who ought to know better have done, that the Samaritans were not already Christians or that they were in some way dispensationally different from all the rest of us. Neither, as we have said, did the apostles ever lay hands on people in order that they should become Christians. They laid hands on them because 'as yet the Spirit was fallen *upon* none of them . . .'

The result of this laying on of hands was that they 'received the Spirit (no article), something which Simon the sorcerer immediately recognized as a possible new act for his show—obviously something to be 'seen and heard'.

Cornelius' friends

Here as with Philip in the city of Samaria, Peter preached Jesus, his death and resurrection, and as he preached 'the Holy Spirit fell *upon* all them which heard the word' (Acts 10:44). How did Peter and his

Jewish friends know that this had happened? 'They heard them speak with tongues, and magnify God'. Peter added that they should be baptized in water because they had 'received the Holy Spirit as well as we', i.e. as they had done at Pentecost. (I gather the double article is used in the Greek of this passage, i.e. 'the Holy the Spirit', but Bullinger insists this is done for dramatic emphasis . . . I am not competent to comment.) In any case, if it were not slightly sacrilegious to comment, one might consider it very strange to think of a person falling on a group of Gentiles!

The Ephesian dozen

Paul's initial question as he arrives in Ephesus is fascinatingly important: 'Did you receive the Holy Spirit when (or since) you believed?' (Acts 19:2, RSV). Remember that Paul had a highly trained intellect, was a most logical thinker, and in any case, this passage is part of the inspired word of God, and therefore the question so worded could only have been asked if there was the possibility of a positive or a negative answer. Otherwise it was a nonsense. Further, 'When you believed' in NT language means only one thing—'when you became a real Christian'. The fact that when he asked the question he did not know that they were not real believers in no way alters the validity of what I am saying. To Paul, 'to believe' meant to have the Spirit of Christ living within (see Rom 8:9) so he could not have been asking whether they were Christians or not. His question establishes the fact that regeneration is not the same as 'receiving the Spirit'. Or, to put it positively, there is a further experience of the Holy Spirit after regeneration. Ideally, it should take place at the same time as regeneration (or momentarily afterwards); but even then, they remain two separate activities of the

Spirit.

To conclude the story of the Ephesian dozen, it turned out that they were not even regenerate. Paul therefore goes on to remedy that, and as a result, baptizes them in water. Thereafter he laid hands on them and the Holy Spirit came '*upon*' them—and they spoke in tongues and prophesied.

The coming 'upon' in the Old Testament

The coming 'upon' of the Spirit may be regarded as the distribution of tools to get the jobs done. The way that this happened and the purpose for which it was given in the Old Testament will therefore give us insights into its continuing purposes in the New Testament.

The seventy elders

> And I will take of the Spirit which is upon thee, and will put it upon them; and they shall bear the burden of the people with thee, that thou bear it not thyself alone (Num 11:17).

The children of Israel, not long out from Egypt fell to complaining and lusting after the food which they had enjoyed in captivity; fish, cucumbers, melons, leeks, onions and garlic, which apparently had been in ample supply.

The full force of their complaints weighed very heavily on Moses so much so that he complained to God saying, 'Wherefore hast thou afflicted thy servant . . . why should I have to act as a nursing father?' and adding, 'I am not able to bear all this people alone'. He even speaks of asking God to finish his life if it had to go on like this.

Today, with a congregation only a fraction of the size of the children of Israel many a pastor or vicar must have similar feelings, if not quite so drastic, as they seek conscientiously to fulfil all the ministries of apostle, prophet, evangelist, pastor and teacher, all rolled into one!

God's answer to this situation now is the same as then: 'Gather unto me seventy men of the elders of Israel . . . and I will take of the spirit which is *upon* thee, and will put it *upon* them; and they shall bear the burden of the people with thee, that thou bear it not thyself alone' (Num 11:16–17).

When this happened, and the Spirit rested upon these seventy, they all began to prophesy. John tells us that the testimony of Jesus is the Spirit of prophesy; and the fascinating part of this story is that two of the seventy were not together with the others when the Spirit fell upon them but elsewhere in the camp; they nonetheless began to prophesy! When Joshua heard this he asked Moses to stop them. Moses reveals the grace of leadership and prophetic insight when he re-buffs Joshua's suggestion: 'Enviest thou for my sake? would God that all the Lord's people were prophets, and that the Lord would put his spirit *upon* them!'

That is exactly what God has done in the new covenant, for Peter says that this coming upon is for 'as many as the Lord our God shall call', i.e. all the Lord's people, and Paul adds, 'ye may all prophesy'.

A major purpose of the coming upon of the Spirit is to distribute tools for the jobs to as many in the body of Christ as are willing to be available to work. There is a great need today, as at the beginning, for God's servants in full time ministry to be relieved of many jobs that keep them from giving themselves to prayer and the ministry of the word (see Acts 6).

The whole concept of the church being the body of Christ is that like a human body every member has a function to fulfil and if that function is missing or ineffectively done the whole body feels the impact—it is sick. A tooth is a very small part of a human body but toothache can disrupt life altogether while it lasts. And kidney failure is often lethal. This underlines the importance of the fact that in both Romans 12 and 1 Corinthians 12, the two chapters dealing with the gifts of the Spirit, the apostle teaches about the body of Christ and the various members eyes, hands, ears, etc.

What a happy healthy and outgoing church is the one that has a shared anointed leadership!

Samson

> And the Spirit of the Lord came mightily upon him, and he rent him [the lion] as he would have rent a kid, and he had nothing in his hand . . . And the Spirit of the Lord came upon him, and he went down to Ash-ke-lon, and slew thirty men of them, and took their spoil . . . And when he came unto Le-hi, the Philistines shouted against him: and the Spirit of the Lord came mightily upon him, and the cords that were upon his arms became as flax that was burned with fire, and his bands loosed from off his hands (Judg 14:6, 19; 15:14).

In the time of Samson the Philistines, a type of Satan and the world, had dominion over Israel. And so there was considerable need for personal deliverance.

Peter tells us that the devil goes about as a roaring lion seeking whom he may devour. These sort of things don't change over the years! A young lion roared against Samson.

God's provision in such a dangerous situation was then as now: 'The Spirit of the Lord came mightily upon him'. He tore the lion asunder as he would have rent a kid, and 'he had nothing in his hand'.

Our trouble, so often, is that we insist on having

something in our hand. Some human weapon, but the weapons of our warfare are not worldly, that is they are not human abilities, but have divine power to the pulling down of strongholds.

'Strongholds' is a very expressive word. We often, alas, allow Satan to get a stronghold on us, in one way or another. We wrestle not against flesh and blood, but against wicked spirits—these are in heavenly places. So beware! That is the very place where we are blessed with all spiritual blessings. The Spirit of the Lord can come upon us mightily to deal with every roaring lion.

Saul

> And the spirit of the Lord will come upon thee, and thou shalt prophesy with them, and shalt be turned into another man (1 Sam 10:6).

This is a favourite passage of mine. It underlines so many of the good things God has for his people in the outpouring of the Holy Spirit.

Not only did Saul prophesy when the Spirit of the Lord came upon him but also 'he was changed into another man and God gave him another heart'. When despised and spoken against he held his peace; and when his friends wanted to wreak revenge, he would have none of it.

But the main transformation was in his being changed from an ordinary man into a king. He was transformed into royalty and able to lead his people into victory against the enemy.

There is no better story in the Bible to illustrate the purpose of the coming upon of the Spirit than the story of Saul; and yet what a sad ending. The word of God is always true to life and never hides the dark sides of human experience.

Pride and disobedience were his downfall—and of

many others since. The desires of the flesh lust against the Spirit and the desires of the Spirit lust against the flesh; 'these are contrary the one to the other: so that ye cannot do the things that ye would. But if ye be led of the Spirit ye are not under the law' (Gal 5:17–18). Beloved now we are the sons of God—a royal priest-hood and it doth not yet appear what we shall be! . . . We are kings and can reign in life—and not lose our royalty.

David

> Then Samuel took the horn of oil, and anointed him in the midst of his brethren: and the Spirit of the Lord came upon David from that day forward (1 Sam 16:13).

As soon as Saul fell and lost his anointing God had David ready to take his place. In our day, if we fall thank God he will not replace us but will restore us by his grace.

All that was true for Saul happened again for David and the Spirit of the Lord came upon David from that day forward. He made his mistakes and more than once sinned grievously but he never lost his anointing or his royalty. In addition his anointing enabled him to be the greatest man of praise of all time.

Elisha

> And it came to pass, when they were gone over, that Elijah said unto Elisha, Ask what I shall do for thee, before I be taken away from thee. And Elisha said, I pray thee, let a double portion of thy spirit be upon me (2 Kings 2:9).

The symbolism here is mighty and inspiring, illustrating our Lord's promise when he said 'the works that I do shall he do also—and greater works' (Jn 14:12).

Elijah, the old prophet is a type of our Lord and

Elisha the young prophet the type of each one of us. The young prophet asked for and received a double portion of the Spirit of the old prophet to be upon him. A double portion does not merely mean twice as much numerically but is a phrase commonly used in the Old Testament to indicate the portion or privilege of the firstborn. Christ is *the* firstborn and has made us co-heirs with himself. Hence the upshot can be in our case as it was with this young prophet, 'The Spirit of Elijah doth rest on Elisha.'

This is exactly symbolic of what it means to be truly baptized with the Holy Spirit. The same Spirit that came upon Jesus as he came out of Jordan is to fall upon us. 'You will receive the power of the Spirit coming upon you . . . and you will be the evidence of me' (a literal translation of 'ye shall be witnesses unto me').

The experience of each of these five Old Testament people, or groups of people, illustrates some aspect of the purpose of the coming upon in the New Testament. Notice:

1. All are for action, i.e. miracle and/or ministry.
2. The action is usually associated with words; words of faith and very often prophecy.
3. In the Old Testament they were given to special people for special jobs. In the New Testament we are all special people and all have special jobs to do!

4
The Nature of Spiritual Gifts

In Denmark, where I have often ministered for many years, spiritual gifts are called *nadegavene* literally 'grace-gifts' and that is exactly right. They are instruments, tools to express and minister the grace of the Lord Jesus Christ in all its fullness. They are given to enable our Lord to continue 'to do and to teach' what he began to do whilst on earth in the flesh. The gifts are the indwelling Christ at work through a Christian; the risen Christ exercising his Lordship over and through the church which is his body.

The gifts are spiritual

Because the gifts are spiritual it follows that:

They are not natural abilities

The gift of tongues, for instance, has no relationship to linguistic knowledge or ability. Neither has interpretation. The gift of the word of knowledge has no relevance to human intellect or capability. That is, the gifts are not mental. Neither are they psychic or soulish.

These other powers of human personality are of course God-given and good and are to be dedicated to the Lord for his control and use. They often have a part to play in the operation of a spiritual gift but they are not *the source of spiritual ministry*. For instance, when prophesying one's mind is being used, but is not the source of the content of the prophecy.

Conybeare makes a strong point to emphasize that the exercise of spiritual gifts was a matter of ordinary occurrence in the early church. He says: 'These miraculous powers are not even mentioned by the apostolic writers as a class apart (as we should now consider them) but are joined in the same classification with other gifts which we are wont to term natural endowments or "talents".'

I am not quite sure whether Conybeare is making the point that the gifts of 'administrative usefulness' and the 'faculty of government' are merely *natural talents* dedicated to God and used by the Holy Spirit or that these, along with healing and tongues, fall into the same category as charisms. He continues, however, that 'It is desirable that we should make a division between the two classes of gifts, the extraordinary and the ordinary although the division was not made by the apostles at the time when both kinds of gifts were in ordinary use.'

Whichever way Conybeare is trying to argue, surely the truth is that in the church such ministries as administration and government should be spiritual ministries —charisms—drawing their ability from the Holy Spirit and not from natural talent. How far we have departed from this ideal is often illustrated by the sad and sometimes bitter arguments and disagreements found in Parochial Church Councils, synods and councils at all levels.

One does not have to have a high IQ rating or be well educated or culturally refined to be used in the gifts of the Spirit. One does have to know how to be responsive to the control of the Holy Spirit.

There is a well-known story of Paganini, the great violinist who came on stage to give a solo recital. As he tuned his violin a string broke; as he continued, another broke; and finally a third one went the same way. He then addressed his audience and said: 'Now see what music one string can produce when in the hands of Paganini.' Similarly God can use one-string-people for the manifestation of spiritual gifts or four-string-people —Peters as well as Pauls.

They are not alternatives to the fruits of the Spirit

Nowhere in the epistles is there the slightest suggestion that the fruits of the Spirit are an alternative to or superior to the gifts of the Spirit. We are to 'follow after charity and desire spiritual gifts'. Conybeare translates this phrase: 'follow earnestly after love; yet delight in the spiritual gifts'.

David du Plessis has a novel, naïve and yet perhaps correct way of interpreting the closing verse of 1 Corinthians 12, 'But covet earnestly the best gifts: and yet show I unto you a more excellent way.' David suggests that the 'more excellent way' the way of love, is a more excellent way of coveting the best gifts! He certainly has a point!

We must, however, face the sad truth that the gifts of the Spirit can be—and often are—in use along with carnality both in the life of those used to exercise the gifts and those in the local church in question. This is nothing new. The moral behaviour of those in the Corinthian church leaves very much to be desired, yet the apostle acknowledges not only that they spoke in tongues far too much, but also that they 'came behind in no gift'.

In this situation the apostle does not suggest that they should no longer exercise spiritual gifts; but rather that they amend their ways and use their gifts properly, warning them of the danger of being merely 'sounding brass and tinkling cymbals'. Perhaps all this has to do with the fact that 'the gifts (*charismata*) and calling of God are without repentance' (Rom 11:29). Jonah ran away and Samson played around with a prostitute, yet neither lost his former gift. This of course is no excuse for laxity in the matter of holy living. Gifts may be exercised if associated with carnality but to what effect? They cannot, I am sure, carry much conviction or spiritual power—if any.

We may look further into the nature of spiritual gifts by considering five Greek words used in 1 Corinthians 12:

Pneumatikos. This is used in verse 1 as a noun although it is really an adjective, and underlines the spiritual nature of the whole discourse extending to the end of chapter fourteen. It means 'of the Spirit'.

Charismata (the plural of *charisma*). This is used in verses 4, 9, 30, and 31, and relates to the grace content. A 'charism' is that which contains and then pours out the *charis* of God. Remember always that the *charisma* of God is eternal life through Jesus Christ our Lord (Rom 6:23)—the greatest *charisma* of all.

Diakonia. This is used in verse 5 translated in the AV 'administrations' and basically means a ministry or a service—a 'usefulness', to borrow Conybeare's word.

Energemata. This word is used in verse 6 and is translated 'operations'. It is from this word that we have our English word 'energy'. This is its basic meaning: *an inworking*. The same Greek root

44

word is often used in the NT translated in the AV as 'effectual' meaning that which causes an effect. Notice especially: 'Whereof I was made a minister (*diakonos*) according to the gift (*dorea*—a present—not *charisma*) of the grace of God given unto me by the *effectual* working of his power' (Eph 3:7); '. . . which every joint supplieth, according to the *effectual* working in the measure of every part' (Eph 4:16); 'he that wrought *effectually* in Peter . . . the same was mighty in me' (Gal 2:8).

This same word in its verb form is also used in 1 Corinthians 12:6 and 11; it is translated in the AV as 'worketh', and that is the basic nature of the *charismata*: they work, they cause effects, or an 'event' as Thomas Smail would say; they cause things to happen. This relates to what we have written elsewhere about what Jesus began to do, and that which our hands have handled of the word of life.

Phanerosis. This is used in verse 7 translated 'manifestation'. The purpose of the exercise of spiritual gifts is to make visible and tangible that the Holy Spirit is at work, causing things to happen that can be 'seen and heard'—i.e. things that are manifest.

Illustrated by the human body

In both chapters where St Paul deals with spiritual gifts (1 Cor 12 and Rom 12) he then goes on to illustrate the use of gifts by the metaphor of the human body.

The main lesson of the human body is that it is a whole, a unity, but in diversity. One control, many functions, many manifestations. They are all interdependent and co-operative—quite incredibly so. Just think of driving a car for instance. The eyes are focused on the road, the hands on the steering wheel, the feet at the pedals, the ears alert and the whole body sitting comfortably. Every member of the body doing its own thing—and how different the 'things' all are—and yet altogether in perfect harmony and co-operation in the one overall purpose. Using the same illustration of driving a car, we can see immediately how stupid and disastrous it is for the hands to say to the feet 'I have no need of you' or similarly the eyes to the ears.

Such is the nature of the body of Christ and also the nature of the differing gifts of the Spirit. Each one is interdependent, not only with the other gifts but also with every ministry and office in the church. The gifts are not to the exclusion of teaching or above the authority of leadership.

Further they are related to function, as are the members of our human body. What use for instance is a knee when one is listening to an orchestra? Or the gift of healing when addressing a 'varsity sports club?

If there is too much of any one gift, as tongues at Corinth, then the whole balance of the body is forfeited. As someone has said about the average church today, 'Instead of a body it has become one big mouth and many small bottoms!'

Usage of the gifts

Gifts are to be exercised according to the proportion of faith, and the grace given to each person being used in this ministry (Rom 12:3, 6).

Each one has to think soberly of himself and his function. It is so easy for some of the 'manifest' gifts to think that they can run the whole outfit; for those who minister healing or who prophesy to think that their gift is all that is necessary for a healthy church. This is sheer pride, and pride is an abomination to the Lord; it is here that carnality intrudes so easily and if unchecked will take over, so much so that grace and faith are quite obliterated.

Each phrase in Romans 12 carries a very practical lesson in the matter of usage: 'let us wait on our ministering' . . . 'with simplicity' . . . 'with diligence' . . . 'with cheerfulness' . . . 'without dissimulation' . . . 'without pretence or hypocrisy' . . . 'but totally genuine . . . in honour preferring one another'.

Because gifts are to be exercised according to the proportion of faith it follows that one is to start small and mature in growth. To start speaking as a child, and mature to talk like a man. George Müller is reputed to have had faith initially for sixpence; but ultimately for thousands of pounds.

One of the problems with the healing ministry is that, for a variety of reasons beyond his control, the one with the gift is usually confronted with sick people who have tried every other means to be healed first and come to the Lord as a last resort, willing, as they say, to try anything once. This means they are probably already very advanced in their sickness. One needs a tremendous amount of faith to pray effectively for an advanced cancer patient.

On the basis of the partnership of the Holy Spirit (see chapter six) the operation of a gift is related to personality. This is as it should be, and it is pathetic to see someone trying obviously to copy somebody else— usually some well-known preacher. The church needs Barnabas—son of consolation—as well as Peter and Paul. His ministry is absolutely essential to meet the needs of many timid souls who are vexed with perplexing anxieties and fears.

In the operation of spiritual gifts it is essential always to remember that they are to be *under control*. First and foremost under the control of the Holy Spirit. Gifts are well defined as the manifestation of the Spirit. It is important to notice that it is the manifestation of the Spirit and not the manifestation of the gift. It is sad and destructive of any anointing to see or hear a person trying to operate a gift without the Lordship of the Spirit being in control.

Under the Spirit's overall control, however, God has ordained that the spirits of the prophets are subject to the prophets. It is to emphasize this by contrast that Paul starts the twelfth chapter of 1 Corinthians by saying: 'Ye know that ye were Gentiles, carried away unto these dumb idols, even as *ye were led*'; and writing to Timothy he insists that God has given us the spirit of love and *a sound mind*. We are not to be overpowered but empowered.

Another aspect of usage is that spiritual gifts can be dormant and need 'stirring up' (2 Tim 1:6–7). I remember praying for a woman in Montreal who had previously been much used of the Lord in many ways, whose gift of prophecy had been allowed to dry up completely. She was deeply repentant and God graciously restored her ministry—much to the benefit of her own health amongst other things!

Gifts are always related to function. They are tools for the job. A bagful of the plumbing tradesman's tools are quite useless for an electrical failure. So also with spiritual gifts. For the evangelist the gift of healing and prophetic words of knowledge; for the pastor the discerning of spirits and words of wisdom plus prophecy that edifies, exhorts and comforts; for the teacher, a word of knowledge. Obviously there is overlapping here and in a modern context when often a vicar or a pastor is expected to fulfil all the functions in the body of Christ one man will be endued with many differing gifts at different times, in different circumstances. There is considerable evidence that the early apostles exercised all the gifts and offices at different times. Apostles have never been withdrawn from the body of Christ and we may expect the same thing to happen again in the fullness of time.

There are two final points about usage which perhaps overshadow all the rest in importance.

Firstly, when Jesus was witnessing to the woman at the well and when the early Christians went everywhere (being scattered through persecution) and when the apostles travelled in what we would now call missionary activity—in all these cases of outreach it is obvious that the manifestation of the Spirit was evident through the gifts of the Spirit. It is a great pity that we have largely confined the gifts to the vicarage house group type of meeting and charismatic Sunday morning worship services.

D. L. Moody was asked if he would give a talk defending the Bible. 'Defend the Bible?' he retorted. 'I would as soon defend an imprisoned lion—open the cage and let it out!' One feels the same about these wonderful manifestations of the power of the risen Christ. Which leads to the second point.

Everything that the Holy Spirit does has the ultimate purpose of glorifying Christ, exalting his name. The sort of prophecy we are lacking is that which causes unbelieving men to fall on their faces and worship God, reporting that God is in us 'of a truth' (1 Cor 14:24–25).

We now address ourselves to ask how the gifts of the Spirit are distributed.

If we accept the view that each Spirit-baptized believer has the Holy Spirit within and the anointing upon him or her, and therefore has the potential of any or all of the gifts already resident, then there is no further question to answer. We may notice however, even taking this view, that in practice it is mostly one (though it may possibly be more) particular gift that is used by any one person most of the time, depending upon their setting in the body and their ministry. This is due largely to the fact that the usage of gifts develops with experience and the growth of faith.

This view, with which I have a lot of sympathy, is not, however, widely held and is even less acted upon in current practice. It is far more common for us to take a literal view of the phrase 'for to one is given', meaning that from then on that person has that gift. How then does that person receive that gift?

Gifts develop

Gifts develop especially when sincerely and humbly coveted and more particularly when it is painfully obvious to the person in question that he/she is sadly in need of such a gift in performing whatever ministry they are called into. This sense of need can be strongest at the time of the initial call into such ministry, or may develop as the ministry develops, or its failure becomes obvious.

The gifts are at the disposal of the Holy Spirit himself, 'dividing to every man severally as he wills'. Two things emerge from this. Firstly, if God has called you into a particular ministry, then obviously the Spirit wills you to have his enablement for that ministry. Secondly, the Spirit distributes, but we must be open to receive and exercise a little receiving faith, especially faith to *begin* in the exercise of the gift in question.

By apostolic ministry

'I long', says the apostle to the Roman church, 'to see you, that I may impart unto you some spiritual gift' (Rom 1:11). This is to the end that they may '*be estab-*

lished'.

It is not wise to try and be too specific as to just how an apostle imparts a gift. It springs no doubt from his premier office in the body of Christ. He will be made aware of what to do first by the Spirit's general guidance, coupled with an inner 'word of knowledge'. Many think that apostles are normally endued with all of the gifts in the course of their ministry.

Such revelation will probably then be expressed in prophecy or by the laying on of hands—and usually both.

Paul had ministered to Timothy by the laying on of hands (2 Tim 1:6). Also Timothy had received a gift by prophecy and the laying on of hands by the presbytery (1 Tim 4:14). Whether these were two different occasions relating to two different gifts or whether the presbytery joined the apostle in the laying on of hands at one time for the giving of one gift is not clear. I would think there were two occasions and (two or more) gifts were involved. In any case we may add a third category.

By the laying on of hands

This, as we have seen, may be done by either the apostle alone, or the apostle plus the presbytery, or the latter alone.

By prophecy

We have already noticed that prophecy often accompanies—usually preceding it—the laying on of hands; and nearly always hands will be laid on by way of confirming or sealing any prophecy.

Gift-giving prophecy should be expected only from either apostles or prophets, and not through the ministry of the *gift of prophecy*. In some circles an acknowledged prophet will actually name in a public gathering an individual in prophecy and the gift that is to be given to that individual. However, I once saw, in Detroit, a variation of this which I thought was much wiser and healthier.

To what we would now call a Renewal Centre, Christians, both those young in the faith and the more mature, would come from a wide area all over the USA and Canada. On arrival the visitor would be accommodated in the home of a resident Christian and counselled by the leaders to fast for a while. When either the leaders or the person thought he or she had sought the Lord with fasting long enough, then at a public worship service, free in the Spirit, such a person would be invited to the front and the leaders would gather round as he knelt in prayer. After quietly waiting on the Lord, one with a prophetic gift would say that he sensed the Lord wanted to give such and such a gift to this person. The others in the ring would wait on the Lord and usually they would agree (possibly adding another gift or some word of explanation, encouragement or warning). Then when they were all satisfied that that was the mind of the Lord they would all lay hands on the person with prayer.

On one occasion I remember a Mr D, already an ordained minister of some years standing, being ministered to in this way. He received the gift of healing and a special mention was made that he would be used in cancer cases. Immediately after the confirmation of the gift all those with cancer in a very large congregation were invited to the front for the application of this newly-given gift. That is putting faith into action!

We must now turn our attention to *abuses*.

Abuses

(1) The main abuse in a modern context is not abuse but *non-use*! We have substituted human ability, theological training, psychology, organizing skills and personality in the place of spiritual gifts.

The well-known words of the prophet Zechariah are relevant here: 'Not by might, nor by power, but by my spirit, saith the Lord.' The word for 'might' used here indicates organizing skill; it is a military word. 'Power' has a personal flavour with it and suggests the personality cult, which is very common amongst us especially in relation to preachers. The world has stolen our Bible word—hardly ever heard before the charismatic renewal!—namely 'charisma', to describe the sort of power here referred to by the prophet. God can harness such power of course, but the spiritual charismata are God's real provision. Worldly charisma is no substitute for the real charisma of the Spirit.

(2) Gifts of the Spirit are not to be *used as toys or playthings* for the enjoyment of charismatic prayer groups.

(3) Gifts in no way give any basis for *thinking one is particularly holy* and are certainly not a basis for thinking that those without such gifts are second-class Christians. Spiritual pride is probably the worst sort of pride, but any sort of pride is objectionable and an abomination in the eyes of the Lord.

(4) There is a lot of confusion caused by the *failure to distinguish between the two different kinds of tongues* (see chapter six). This not only causes confusion but is also a sound basis for a lot of opposition to tongues as a whole. The fact that a person is able to speak in tongues is no reason on its own for this to happen in public.

Also the manner in which some people speak in tongues in public is occasionally very off-putting and quite wrong.

(5) I was just about to write that *the exclusively private use of the gifts* i.e. in little private huddles, is not good and can lead to all kinds of trouble, when my front door bell rang and an old acquaintance arrived. He was just full of how the Lord had blessed him and his wife in guidance and worry-free living through a ministry between them of tongues and interpretation. I must say his story was most interesting and convincing.

But this is just one more illustration of a very basic truth, that God always answers real faith, and that a vital faith can carve out its own pattern, often in new and novel ways.

But this in no way leads me away from insisting that the private use of the gifts is generally to be deplored and avoided (see 2 Pet 1:20).

(6) Finally, a note about *new wine in old wineskins*. Here is a real problem, inasmuch as it is often almost impossible to make room in the established orders of service for the exercise of spiritual gifts.

This is a major problem but it is no excuse at all for anyone who has a spiritual gift to bulldoze their way into an established order of service and particularly not against the wish (and maybe theology) of the vicar or minister. God is a God of order and grace and we are to respect very highly those whom God has set over us in the Lord, and be at peace among ourselves (1 Thess 5:13).

Some seem to think that they must speak in tongues (or prophesy) in every meeting they attend as a kind of witness. This is abuse. If God has placed you in a fellowship where as yet the gifts are not manifest, then a meek and quiet spirit is called for—a manifestation of the gracious spirit of the Master, an expression of the joy of the Lord and victorious godly living. This will witness far more effectively than any bulldozing activity which in all probability at the same time will give the impression that one thinks one is a superior Christian and the rest of the congregation second-class.

The manifestation of the Spirit that is given to every man is for the common good—remember it is the manifestation of the Spirit and not the manifestation of the gift.

5
Pentecost

Pentecost changed everything. Before then the disciples were already regenerate, with the Holy Spirit living within them, otherwise Jesus would never have called them 'brethren' (Jn 20:17). Further, he had also breathed upon them and said 'Receive ye the Holy Spirit' (Jn 20:22).

They had actually seen the risen Lord. He had repeated for them a former miracle of the draft of fishes, he had eaten with them and given them many infallible proofs of his resurrection. He taught them about the kingdom of God and yet they were still scared to death for fear of the Jews. They were fearful and useless.

After Pentecost they were completely new men and women. They were bold, no longer fearful; full of dynamic and power and not useless. They were new men, had new power, had a new Bible, a new witness and immediately entered into a new warfare. They also entered into a new fellowship, quite unique and never known before. Everything was changed.

God's purpose of a personal Pentecost for all his

people throughout all the church age is exactly the same as it was initially. Few enough manifest such dramatic change, but this in no way negates God's purpose. Further, without being quite so dramatic, there are many living examples of a quite remarkable transformation as a result of a personal Pentecost.

The last words of Jesus before he ascended spelt out clearly the meaning of what was to happen not many days hence. Already Jesus had equated 'the promise of the Father' with 'power from on high'. Now, drawing a parallel with John's baptism with water he specifically defines 'the promise of the Father' as being baptized with the Holy Spirit, spelling it out in detail as follows: 'But ye shall receive power, after that the Holy Ghost is come upon you: and ye shall be witnesses unto me both in Jerusalem, and in all Judaea, and in Samaria, and unto the uttermost part of the earth.' A more correct translation of the first part of this quotation is as follows: 'but ye shall receive the power of the Holy Spirit coming upon you'.

First, noting the preposition 'upon', let us further see exactly what our Lord was saying:

Ye shall receive power

The Greek word is *dunamis*, as everyone knows, and from which we derive our English word 'dynamite'. Inasmuch as the Holy Spirit always speaks of and uplifts Christ rather than himself, this power is the same as that which the apostle refers to when he wrote to the Corinthians: 'Most gladly therefore will I rather glory in my infirmities, that the power of Christ may rest upon me . . . for when I am weak then am I strong' (2 Cor 12:9–10). This strength manifested itself in signs and wonders and mighty deeds, albeit also in much patience, involved in spending and being spent for others (see 2 Cor 12:9–15).

Writing to the Colossians the apostle refers not only to *dunamis* power, but also *kratos* namely dominion and *exousia* which is authority (see Col 1:11–13). These are all related and should all result from a coming upon of power from on high.

Ye shall be witnesses

This is basically something we are to *be* rather than something we are to *do*. The whole concept has, I feel, been considerably watered down by making it read 'witnesses *for* me'. It is '*unto me*'. What does this mean?

The word 'witness' may legitimately be translated 'evidence'. This, I think, is the most fundamental concept of what Pentecost is for. When you receive the power of the Holy Spirit coming upon you, Jesus is saying, you will be the evidence of me. The evidence that I am alive, glorified and ascended; still the same as ever, continuing all those things which I began both to do and to teach whilst I was with you in the flesh.

We are all familiar with the idea of a person being a wet blanket. When such a person comes into the room the social temperature immediately drops several degrees. A true witness of Christ ought to be the exact opposite of a wet blanket. As a witness enters a room everyone ought to be aware that Christ is now amongst them.

The thought is allied to the whole purpose of the corporate body of Christ. A major function of a human body is as a means of location. We all on occasions take refuge in the phrase 'I will be with you in spirit' when we do not wish to be there in person. But it is a falsehood. It is our body alone that locates where we are. That is a major function of the church which is his body. If you want to contact Christ, you will find him where his body is to be found. It is so for each one of us as his witness.

See and hear

> Therefore being by the right hand of God exalted, having received of the Father the promise of the Holy Ghost, he hath shed forth this, which ye now see and hear (Acts 2:33).

In modern times a witness is usually somebody called to a legal court. The essential requirement of such a person is that he has seen and heard for himself; his evidence must be personal and firsthand.

This is essential if we are to witness effectively for Christ. A second-hand story can help but what we have seen and heard ourselves is most effective, and is calculated to defeat any theological contrary argument.

John begins his first epistle on this vein: 'That . . . which we have heard, which we have seen with our eyes . . . and our hands have handled, of the Word of life' (1 Jn 1:1).

For many years as a preacher I had to rely on *A Thousand Tales Worth Telling* and similar books to supply my illustrations of what God was doing and wanting to do. I am deeply grateful to God that there came a day when that was no longer necessary. I could tell what I myself had seen and heard and my own hands had handled of the word of life. At that time my own life and ministry were transformed.

Witnesses

The Greek word for witness is *martus* from which we get our English word martyr. It now carries with it the thought of death. And indeed, the basic purpose of Pentecost was and is that we should die in favour of the

Lord Christ himself. Calvary and Pentecost must always be intimately connected.

The fundamental truth of the well-known verse of Galatians 2:20, where it says 'I am crucified with Christ: nevertheless I live; yet not I, but Christ liveth in me . . .', is possible only in the enabling of the power of Pentecost. God's provision for us to live in the reality of Galatians 2:20 is Acts 1:8 and its implied, 'I am to die in favour of the Lord.' That is why and how the apostle can say 'for me to live is Christ' (to live). That is also why he prays that 'Christ may dwell in your hearts by faith . . . that ye might be filled with all the fulness of God . . . and prove that he is able to do exceeding abundantly above all that we ask or think, according to the power that worketh in us' (see Eph 3:17–20).

Partnership

'They entered into a new fellowship' we have written at the start of this chapter, 'quite unique and never known before.' This was the great *koinonia* the communion of the Holy Spirit mentioned in the grace of 2 Corinthians 13:14.

This has great relevance to our community—the body of Christ as evidenced in Acts 2:41–47. A well-known book has called Pentecost 'nine o'clock in the morning'. Perhaps we may refer to the communion as six o'clock in the evening.

But the more fundamental meaning of *koinonia* is related to its meaning of partnership with the Holy Spirit. This we have fully developed in the chapter on speaking in tongues (chapter six), so all that needs to be said here is that the partnership consists of his ability working with and expressing itself through our human personality with all its faculties of body and soul.

Receiving your personal Pentecost

Here we sail in controversial waters though, one is glad
to report, much less controversial than some twenty
years ago. Undoubtedly the experience of hundreds of
thousands of Christians all over the world in every denomination has largely taken the ground from under
the feet of those who claim that one receives everything
at regeneration and that therefore a later, or at least a
different, experience of the Holy Spirit is invalid.

I do not propose to get deeply involved in this controversy save to assert that obviously I am fully convinced from Scripture, personal experience and observation, that there is a separate experience of the Holy
Spirit, always a personal Pentecost for all God's
people.

There has been disagreement, if not controversy, as
to what such an experience should be called. When
Michael Harper and I took the message of the charismatic movement (as it was initially called) to Denmark
we were quickly met by a delegation of leaders asking
that we avoid all use of the word baptism in relation to
being baptized with the Holy Spirit. Michael graciously
refused to accede to their request on the ground that it
was the phrase our Lord himself used and we could not
therefore jettison it.

The reason for the Danish request was that there had
been so much division and bitterness over baptism in
water that they feared that it would all be resuscitated if
we used the phrase 'baptism in the Spirit'. However we
promised that whenever we did use the word baptism in
relation to the Holy Spirit we would go out of our way
to indicate that it had no relation to water baptism (although in a deeper way of course, it has a relationship
as was shown in the case of the Spirit falling upon our

Lord as he came out of the waters of the Jordan).

To return to terminology. Jesus called it being 'baptized with the Spirit'. It is perhaps significant that the use of the noun 'baptism' is not to be found in the New Testament. Always the verb.

Today, for their own reasons (largely to do with theological backgrounds) many people prefer to refer to it as being 'filled with the Spirit'. Earlier generations used the phrase 'second blessing'. Today this is best avoided, first because it tends to revive old arguments; secondly because it seems to ignore the fact that our Lord has third, fourth, etc to the nth blessings for us all through our lives.

Even the phrase 'one's personal Pentecost' which we have used to head this section has drawbacks because it can be associated in a wrong way with the historical Pentecostal church, which is fair enough if you have an open, unprejudiced and loving heart but which many find unacceptable.

The first known modern experience in the UK was designated by the Anglican priest the Reverend Boddy of Sunderland as 'the power fell' which has little to be said against it.

Thomas Smail writes on the subject in his *Reflected Glory*, and this is surely the only correct attitude to this abortive discussion:

> As the experience itself is not to be legalised or stereotyped in any way, so the language in which we describe it must not be stereotyped either. We have argued that the term 'baptism in the spirit' when set in its right context is one way in which, in responsibility to Scripture, it can be legitimately described. But there are many others, and the Holy Spirit, amidst all the other realms of his creativity, can be expected to be creative in our theology as well, and as we discuss these things together within the Body of Christ, give us more adequate language with which to de-

pict and praise himself and his work—adequate both to the richness of Scripture and the need and understanding of modern men.

This is Smail's conclusion near the end of his final chapter which is entitled 'By Whatever Name—Receive!', which surely must be our final remark on this controversy.

Before we go on to explore just how one is to receive this baptism, perhaps a sample of quotations from a few distinguished Christians will help to give us encouragement in our quest. First a general quotation. James A. Stewart in his *Heaven's Throne Gift* quotes a man called James A. McConkey as follows:

> I was standing on the wall of a great lock. Outside was a huge lake vessel about to enter. At my feet lay the empty lock—waiting. For what? Waiting to be filled. Way beyond lay great Lake Superior with its limitless abundance of supply, also waiting. Waiting for what? Waiting for something to be done at the lock ere the great lake could pour in its fulness. In a moment it was done. The lock keeper reached out his hand and touched a steel lever. A little wicket gate sprang open under the magic touch, at once the water in the lock began to boil and seethe. As it seethed I saw it rapidly creeping up the walls of the lock. In a few moments the lock was full. The great gates swung open and the huge ship floated into the lock now filled to the brim with the fulness impoured from the waiting lake without.

Now let us hear what Dr Martyn Lloyd-Jones has to say. Writing in the *Westminster Record* in September 1964 he says:

> There is nothing, I am convinced, that so quenches the Spirit as the teaching which identifies the baptism of the Holy Spirit with regeneration. But it is a very commonly held teaching today, indeed it has been the popular view for many years.

They say that the baptism of the Holy Spirit is 'non-experimental', that it happens to everybody at regeneration. So we say 'ah well, I am already baptized in the Holy Spirit, it happened when I was born again, it happened at my conversion: there is nothing for me to seek, I have got it all'.

Got it all? Well, if you have got it all, I simply ask in the name of God why are you as you are? If you have got it all, why are you so unlike those apostles, why are you unlike New Testament Christians? Got it all! Got it all at your conversion! Well, where is it I ask.

Also writing in his recent, well-known book *Joy Unspeakable* (Kingsway 1984) the Doctor has this to say (on page 31): 'But what is established beyond any doubt is that one can be a believer without being baptized by the Holy Spirit.'

Later he adds on the same page:

They are true believers, children of God, but still they have not been baptized with Holy Spirit because we read in verse six (Acts Chapter 19) 'When Paul had laid his hands upon them, the Holy Ghost came on them; and they spake with tongues, and prophesied.'

Now there is an absolute proof that you can be a true believer in the Lord Jesus Christ and still not be baptized with the Holy Spirit; that incident proves it twice over. Twice over! The question at the beginning and what actually happened subsequently. The important point is that there is a difference, that there is a distinction between believing and being baptized with the Holy Spirit.

Now let us hear what John Wesley has to say on this subject. I quote from John Wesley's *Journal*. First of all under the date May 24th 1738:

In the evening I went very unwillingly to a society in Aldersgate Street where one was reading Luther's Preface to the epistle to the Romans. About a quarter before nine, while he was describing the change which God works in the heart through faith in Christ, I felt my heart strangely warmed. I felt I did trust in Christ, Christ alone for salvation; and an assurance was given me that He had taken away *my* sins, even *mine*, and saved *me* from the law of sin and death.

Now I want to quote an entry dated January 1st 1739, that is some six or more months later than his famous 'heart strangely warmed' experience. This is what he writes:

Mr. Hall, Kinchin, Ingham, Whitefield, Hutchins and my brother Charles were present at our lovefeast in Fetter Lane with about sixty of our brethren. About three in the morning, as we were continuing instant in prayer, the power of God came mightily *upon* us, inasmuch as many cried out for exceeding joy, and many fell to the ground. As soon as we were recovered a little from that awe and amazement at the present of His Majesty we broke out with one voice 'We praise thee O God; we acknowledge Thee to be the Lord.'

Everyone is, I suppose, familiar with the first passage relating John Wesley's experience of his heart being strangely warmed, but relatively few, I imagine, are aware of the second experience some months later and quite obviously this was the experience which made John and Charles Wesley into the mighty men of revival that they subsequently were.

Now let us hear the witness of a well-known modern Methodist, namely Samuel Chadwick, the late Principal of Cliff College, Sheffield:

I owe everything to the gift of Pentecost. It came to me when I was not seeking it. I was about my Heavenly Father's business, seeking means whereby I could do the work to which he had called and sent me, and in my search I came across a prophet, heard a testimony, and set out to seek I knew not what. I knew that it was a bigger thing than I had ever known. It came along the line of duty, in a crisis of obedience. When it came I could not explain what had happened, but I was aware of things unspeakable and full of glory. Some results were immediate. There came into my soul a deep peace, a thrilling joy, and a new sense of power. My mind was quickened. I felt that I had received a new faculty of understanding. Every power was vitalised. My bodily powers were quickened. There was a new sense of spring and vitality, a new power of endurance and a strong man's exhilaration in big things. Things began to happen. What we had failed to do by strenuous endeavour came to pass without labour. It was as when the Lord Jesus stepped into the boat that with all their rowing had made no progress, 'immediately the ship was at the land whither they went'. It was gloriously wonderful.

The things that happened were the least part of the experience. The wind and the fire and the tongues excited most comment, but they vanished, and it was the realities that remained that were most wonderful. The experience gave me the key to all my thinking, all my service, and all my life. Pentecost gave me the key to the Scriptures. It has kept my feet in all the slippery places of all sorts of criticism. [*The Way to Pentecost* (Fleming H. Revell, Co.)]

Dr R. A. Torrey writing in his book *Why God used D. L. Moody* has this to say:

The seventh thing that was the secret why God used D. L. Moody was that he had a very definite enduement with power from on high, a very clear and definite 'baptism with the Holy Ghost'; he had no doubt about it. In his early days he was a great hustler; he had a tremendous desire to do something, but he had no real power. He worked very largely in the energy of the flesh. But there were two humble 'Free Methodist' women who used to come over to his meetings in the Y.M.C.A. One was 'Aunty Cook' and the other Mrs. Snow. These two women would come to Mr. Moody at the close of his meetings and say: 'We are praying for you'. Finally Mr. Moody became somewhat nettled and said to them one night: 'Why are you praying for me? Why don't you pray for the unsaved?' They replied, 'We are praying that you may get the power'. Mr. Moody did not know what they meant, but he got to thinking about it, and then went to those women and said: 'I wish you would tell me what you mean' and they told him about the definite baptism with the Holy Ghost. Then he asked that he might pray *with* them and not they merely pray for him.

Aunty Cook once told me of the intense fervour with which Mr. Moody prayed on that occasion. She told me in words that I scarcely dare repeat, though I have never forgotten them. And he not only prayed with them, but he also prayed alone. Not long after, one day on his way to England, he was walking up Wall Street in New York (Mr. Moody very seldom told this and I almost hesitate to tell it) and in the midst of the bustle and hurry of that city, his prayer was answered: the power of God fell upon him as he walked up the street and he had to hurry off to the house of a friend and ask that he might have a room by himself, and in that room he stayed alone for hours; and the Holy Ghost came upon him, filling his soul with such joy that at last he had to ask God to withold his hand, lest he die on the spot from very joy. He went out from that place with the power of the Holy Ghost upon him and when he got to London the power of God wrought through him mightily in North London and hundreds were added to the Church and that was what led to his being invited over for the wonderful campaign that followed in later years.

In concluding these quotations let me give you a paragraph from *Heaven's Throne Gift* by James A. Stewart, referred to earlier, who himself was mightily used in eastern Europe in the early part (I think) of this century. Here is his quotation: 'In conclusion, let us make it clear that there is a vast difference in our possessing the Spirit of God and the Spirit of God possessing us . . . The burning question is, has the Holy Spirit a monopoly of me today?'

So now let us address ourselves to the question, 'How do we receive our personal Pentecost?'

There are three basic requirements before we actually begin to seek. The first, obviously, is a personal knowledge of Christ as Saviour and Lord, or as we have designated it: an experience of the Holy Spirit 'within'. The second is a clear conviction from Scripture that there is such an experience. Thirdly a deep sense of need. The promise of the Spirit in OT language is 'I will pour water on him that is *thirsty*.'

A lot of people seem to take the view that they are open to the Holy Spirit and if God wants to fill them or baptize them then that is okay. Such an attitude is as stupid in relation to the Holy Spirit as it is to being born again. The blessings of Calvary and Pentecost are the same in this respect. Both are available to all, and for all the church age, but both need to be sought with conviction of sin and need respectively, and received simply on the ground of grace through faith.

I knew a man, a lawyer, who went into his church and asserted: 'I am not coming out of here until I am baptized with the Holy Spirit.' His deep sense of need and longing are exemplary, though his method of achieving his aim is somewhat dangerous—chiefly because it can offend the principle of the Lordship of Christ. But that kind of 'thirst' and faith resemble the Syro-Phoenician woman who came to Jesus with her request and refused to be put off even after being treated (apparently) as a Gentile dog. The Lord granted her request—and also that of my lawyer friend.

With a deep sense of thirst and need, then, how do we set about seeking to be filled with the Spirit? There are three main ways, though it is most important not to lay down any specific tram lines for the Spirit to run on. He is like the wind and blows where he will.

Ask and ye shall receive

> If ye then, being evil, know how to give good gifts unto your children: how much more shall your heavenly Father give the Holy Spirit to them that ask him? (Lk 11:13).

It depends largely on how thirsty we are, on our sense of need and how much faith we exercise as to how long our asking may take. It may be short-lived, receiving the answer at a particular time of prayer set apart for this special purpose. Or it may be prolonged as the conviction deepens. It is in this connection that the procedure of 'tarrying' is relevant.

James A. Stewart, the much-used evangelist referred to earlier who saw revival in east Europe early this century, tells how he much respected his evangelical teachers who taught that the baptism which John the Baptist said Jesus would accomplish was fulfilled in the incorporation of the believer into the body of Christ according to 1 Corinthians 12:13. Yet as he studied the word of God for himself, conscious of his faithfulness to evangelical truth, yet without an effective ministry, he became more and more convinced that there was a baptism of power. This, he said, grieved him considerably because he held his teachers in high esteem. But he 'tarried', searching, open and longing, and God met him with supernatural power from on high.

In the 1960s I knew two lady missionaries working in Morocco. They had been friends for years. The elder one, who had spent a lifetime in Morocco came home on leave and was baptized with the Holy Spirit. On returning to Morocco, touched with her new fire and power and enthusiasm for her new experience of the

Holy Spirit, she witnessed to her younger friend of (Plymouth) Brethren background and found only opposition in her friend's attitude even to the point of endangering their long friendship. It was their custom to have a week's holiday together every now and then in Morocco and although their relationship was strained they decided to have a week together as usual.

The elder one persisted in her witness and the younger in her opposition. The atmosphere became unbearable but on the last night before their holiday finished the younger was standing at the door of the kitchen, still arguing when she distinctly heard a voice which called her by name and said, 'You're wrong!' This was so clear, so unmistakable, unexpected and unusual that it shook her. It was late at night. She took her nightcap drink and retired to bed but to little sleep.

Early next morning she caught her bus to return to Casablanca. She lived alone and on returning home she shut herself in till the matter was finalized. She re-read all the traditional books which insisted that 1 Corinthians 12:13 referred to being baptized with the Holy Spirit and decided 'they didn't know what they were talking about' (her own words and a complete volte-face) took a rest on her couch and asked to receive. The power of the Holy Spirit fell upon her and she found herself speaking in tongues and her heart dancing for joy.

I have had the privilege of talking with many, including some clergy, who have simply prayed to receive this experience and have had a glorious answer.

While preaching, the Holy Spirit falls

This was the experience of Peter, related in Acts 10:44–47, as he preached Jesus (N.B. not the Holy Spirit) to the Gentiles in the house of Cornelius. Although the normal order is for people to become Christians, be baptized in water and thereafter to be filled with the Holy Spirit (see Acts 2:38) in this case the order was reversed, underlining how important it is for us not to make any hard and fast rules about procedures.

It is interesting to note also in this case that it is specifically stated by Luke that they knew 'that on the Gentiles also was poured out the gift of the Holy Spirit. *For* (i.e. because) they heard them speak with tongues, and magnify God.' Notice this two-fold evidence. Later in relating the incident to a sceptical synod in Jerusalem Peter says: 'As I began to speak, the Holy Ghost fell on them, as on us at the beginning' (Acts 11:15). Peter then related this baptism to John's baptism in water, just as Jesus himself had done immediately before his ascension.

Years ago, before I set out for a spell of ministry in Canada, the brethren laid hands on me for the Lord's blessing. As they did so a word of prophecy was given over me. The prophecy indicated that I 'would see people (across the Atlantic) running to the Saviour'. I must say in all honesty, I took this promise with the proverbial pinch of salt.

However I was preaching at a convention in Philadelphia (USA) when suddenly I became aware of some disturbance in the congregation. To my amazement I saw six men in different parts of the congregation simultaneously rise to their feet and start literally hastening to the altar at the front of the church. Naturally I finished preaching immediately and went to the altar to minister to these six men. All of them were urgently seeking to be baptized in the Holy Spirit. We laid hands on them and each one received.

That was not exactly as I preached, as in Peter's case, but near enough and an unexpected fulfilment of the prophecy given to me in England.

It is my conviction that a more effective, positive and anointed ministry of the word cuts out a lot of the need for endless counselling and personal ministry afterwards, in relation to many subjects including being baptized in the Holy Spirit—and also healing, deliverance and sanctification.

In the Acts of the Apostles it was normal for people who heard the preaching to do the asking, 'What must I do?' Today so often the preacher has to plead with people to make a response. This is part of the curse of the modern insistence in many quarters on 'sermonettes' which itself is part of a wider modern curse. We are allowed to speak and enjoy fellowship socially but not in church; we are allowed to be enthusiastic about a new car, a new dress, our golf handicap, or football team—anything, except the most important thing of all in life, our Christian experience and our Lord himself.

The laying on of hands

> Then laid they their hands on them, and they received the Holy Ghost (Acts 8:17).

Each time of revival and renewal seems to have one or more special emphases. In the present renewal one such emphasis is the restored ministry of the laying on of hands, which the writer to the Hebrews calls one of the foundational doctrines (Heb 6:2).

In the early church this seems to have been the most usual way in which people received their personal Pentecost, as for instance in the case of the new converts at both Samaria and Ephesus, and of the apostle Paul himself.

Traditionally this ministry has been incorporated into the act of confirmation, where the bishop alone does the laying on of hands and nothing very dramatic is expected to be seen and/or heard at the time of this ordinance.

But recently there has been a considerable upsurge of this ministry in many quarters exercised by a variety of people other than official bishops, ranging from rank and file clergy, ministers, local elders and, in some quarters, to any member of the body of Christ who is already baptized with the Spirit.

The justification for this enlarged ministry is that while it was Peter and John in Samaria and Paul in Ephesus, it was Ananias—an ordinary believer—who was sent by the Lord to lay hands on Saul of Tarsus (as he then was).

One has seen this greatly enlarged ministry used extensively and effectively and it is no time for us to put a damper on any who are seeking to move out in simple faith in this or any other ministry. Nevertheless a little caution is necessary. Indeed Dr Martyn Lloyd-Jones insists, in *Joy Unspeakable*, 'there is a very great danger here' and adds, 'and no man should venture to lay his hand upon another unless he has received a definite and special commission to do so. He must not do it automatically.'

The 'special commission' requirement mentioned by the Doctor was certainly the basis on which Ananias moved. The Lord appeared to him in a vision and gave him specific and detailed instructions as to where to go and on whom to lay his hands. He was quite reluctant to go, which is very understandable considering that Saul had only recently still been 'breathing out threatenings and slaughter against the disciples of the Lord'. Ananias was certainly not like some around today who are only too anxious, on any and every occasion, to lay hands suddenly on all and sundry. This is to be deplored.

We are all looking for NT happenings to be restored in the church; but we also need to remember that the young church was very much alive spiritually and moving in a general atmosphere of what we would today call revival—and unfortunately that is not the case with us. This makes a tremendous difference to many things.

The proof of the rightness of Ananias's action was of course in the outcome—both healing and the infilling of the Spirit for the apostle Paul to be. That must be our criterion too and leaders should keep a critical eye on the results of their sometimes over-enthusiastic encouragement of so called 'body ministry'.

Dr Lloyd-Jones further mentions well-known names of people transformed by being baptized in the Holy Spirit like Jonathan Edwards, John Wesley, George Whitefield, Charles Finney and D. L. Moody as well as R. A. Torrey, Howell Harris and Daniel Rowlands and then adds: 'I do not know of a single incident among such men where they received the blessing as a result of the laying on of hands of someone else; not a single one.'

If I may add a counterbalancing remark, I would again mention that in this renewal the ministry of laying on of hands has been specially restored and given prominence and blessing by the Holy Spirit. Times change and the Scriptures speak of 'present truth' (2 Peter 1:12). As always, let all things be done to edification, and each be fully persuaded in his/her own mind.

I personally had a quite dramatic introduction to this ministry. It happened in Canada before the days of charismatic renewal. The Lord had recently been at work in my life quickening a living and active faith for life and ministry. I was attending a small convention as

74

a very junior speaker in the days when the ministerial hierarchy concept was strong. The night before the big day I was awakened by the Lord (a *very* unusual happening for me!) and made to understand about this ministry of the laying on of hands for receiving the baptism of the Holy Spirit. In my new-found faith I found this completely new concept quite thrilling—until I felt the Lord saying that *tomorrow morning* I was to preach about this and then put it into practice!

Two small things make this story poignant. First it was unheard of that a junior should preach on the big day. Second, it was a revered ritual that we all partook of a turkey dinner in the basement of the church at lunchtime.

I went off to sleep again. In the morning I took my place at the end of the line of preachers in order of preference. The main preacher preached. Turkey dinner time was fast approaching. The President then out of the blue announced that I should preach. My fears vanished. I stood and preached definitely and very shortly from Acts 8, and then invited those who wished to be baptized in the Spirit to come forward for this ministry of the laying on of hands. A dozen people came forward including a couple of ordained ministers. I looked back to my fellow preachers to join me in the ministry but not a soul moved! 'You preached it, you get on with it' filled the atmosphere!! Nothing daunted —for I had heard from the Lord—down I went and laid hands on all twelve one after the other and all twelve received and we were ready for our turkey dinner on time!

6

Tongues and Interpretation

There is an apparent contradiction in Paul's teaching in 1 Corinthians on the subject of 'tongues'. I say 'apparent' because I am sure the Scriptures never contradict themselves.

On the one hand in 1 Corinthians 12:30 he writes: 'Do all speak with tongues?' The obvious answer to this question is no. On the other hand, only a few paragraphs further on he writes: 'I would that ye all spake with tongues' and he supports his wish on their behalf by adding from his own experience: 'I thank my God, I speak with tongues more than ye all' (1 Cor 14:18).

So, why and how is the contradiction only apparent and not real? The answer lies in understanding that there are two kinds of speaking in tongues: one in public and another in private. Do all speak in tongues in public? No. Do, or at least should, all speak in tongues in private? Yes.

I find that a little distinction in terminology quickly dispels this confusion. I confess that my theological friends never seem impressed with my suggestion, nevertheless I find it most helpful when speaking to ordinary Christians who are seeking clarification on the subject.

Therefore, I reserve the phrase *'speaking in tongues'* for that personal *glossolalia* which is available to all as a result of being baptized with the Holy Spirit; and *'the gift of tongues'* for the public use of tongues, which is used always and only in conjunction with the gift of interpretation. Do all exercise the *'gift* of tongues'? No . . . but the scriptural desire is that all shall *speak* with tongues.

If the theologians disagree, so be it (though I cannot see why!); I am not pressing particularly for a *theological* distinction but rather a practical one, an experiential one to help genuine seekers for peace of mind on the subject.

Admittedly there is one objection to the distinction, namely that Paul does not ask: 'Do all speak with the *gift* of tongues?' But the question is in the context of other gifts, namely between healing and interpretation. We may also note that in no case in the book of Acts does it ever read: 'And they all received the gift of tongues.' On the day of Pentecost, for instance it reads: 'they all began to speak in tongues', and that pattern follows right on throughout the book.

A simple definition

On the face of it, there ought to be no need for a definition of something so plain and obvious as speaking in tongues. But there has been so much wild and extravagant thinking on the subject that it is good to see exactly what the Scriptures say when it first occurred on the day of Pentecost: 'They . . . began to speak with other tongues, as the Spirit gave them utterance' (Acts 2:4).

Just that; perfectly simple; neither more nor less. Let us examine it bit by bit.

First notice, it is *they* who began to speak—not the Holy Spirit. This is fundamental, as we shall see later. Moreover, it is because many people seem to be expecting the Holy Spirit to do everything in this operation (including the speaking) that they fail to begin.

Next notice it says, 'They *began* to speak'! Now, there was no need for Luke to put it like that; he could just as easily and more naturally have written, 'and they spoke with tongues'. But God's word in this, as always, is not only precise but also helpful to our weaknesses. A well-known phrase from the commercial world is applicable here: 'The secret of getting on is getting a start.' Often people to whom we have been ministering were obviously being baptized with the Spirit (you can tell when it is happening) and the Spirit was giving them the words (tongues), yet, for a variety of reasons, they have not begun to speak.

There are two main reasons for this failure to begin. The first we have already mentioned, namely that some expect the Spirit somehow to do the speaking—or at least to *make* them speak. The second and very common reason is that Satan cunningly suggests that they are making the words up. This is often quite devastating and especially to the most sincere people who are anxious only for the 'real thing', but in view of the slanderous background to the whole subject throughout history, they are scared to death of any counterfeit.

This gift, like every other gift from the Lord is received 'by grace through faith'. There used to be strong teaching in some (otherwise very good) quarters that one must go through an intensive time of sanctification in preparation for being baptized with the Spirit. There is some truth in this idea, of course, and we will look at it later, but initially, it cannot be too strongly emphasized that this is a gift from the glorified Christ; and as such must be received by grace through faith. If it were given to those who are 'good enough', who would receive?

So, to begin speaking in tongues faith needs to be exercised, preferably unconsciously. That is, one must steadfastly ignore the devil's lie that one is making up the words and believe quite simply that the Holy Spirit is doing exactly what the Bible says he will do, namely, 'give them utterance' i.e. the words. The Greek word translated 'utterance' is actually a verb used as a noun. It is found in Acts 2:14, 'But Peter . . . lifted up his voice, and *said* . . .' and in Acts 26:25, 'I am not mad, most noble Festus; but *speak forth* the words of truth and soberness.' Now, it is possible, of course, to speak using a lot of mumbo-jumbo words, as also by satanic inspiration; but at the sincere moment of seeking and/or being prayed for with (or without) the laying on of hands, one just has to exercise simple faith in what Jesus said about receiving the Spirit, namely that if we ask for an egg, our heavenly Father will not give us a serpent.

One final practical point. It says, they began to *speak*. When ministering to (denominationally) Pentecostal people I emphasize that it does not say, 'began to *shout*'; and when speaking to Anglicans (and the others) I hint that it is not, 'began to *whisper*'!

We shall return to this matter of speaking, but so much for a simple definition: 'they . . . began to speak with other tongues, as the Spirit gave them utterance'.

Do I have to speak in tongues?

This question is heard much less frequently these days

than twenty years ago; but it is still relevant. Before we answer the question, let us first consider the question itself. It is thoroughly negative; the whole concept of the question seems to be wrong. One may with equal relevance ask a dozen other similar questions: Do I have to go to church? Do I have to be baptized? Do I have to attend the sacrament of the Lord's supper?

I suppose in the last resort one may be converted without going to church, without being baptized or attending the sacrament . . . But who that is truly converted *wants* to leave these things out? Similarly, we may believe in the Holy Spirit and seek a definite experience of being baptized with the Spirit without speaking in tongues. But who wants to?

So, why is the question asked? A failure to differentiate between the two kinds of 'tongues' lies at the root of the matter. Paul states: 'Yet in the church I had rather speak five words with my understanding, that by my voice I might teach others also, than ten thousand words in an unknown tongue' (1 Cor 14:19). This is a very important verse, but not relevant to our present enquiry. It has to do only with speaking in tongues *in the church* and is therefore entirely irrelevant as to whether, as an individual, I should speak in tongues or not. The point of Paul's preference is *that he might teach others*. But when one is speaking in tongues in private, there are no others present to be taught!

So, why do people ask the question and apparently seek to be baptized with the Spirit without speaking in tongues? The answer is, because of the historical background to the whole subject. Consider four aspects of this:

Excesses

Just that one word. What a multitude of sins it covers—

or at least, it is used to cover! For, as far as I have ever been able to find out, very few (if any) of the people who hide behind this word have ever been in a meeting where such excesses are supposed to have taken place. 'That such excesses have been committed is undoubtedly true', that well-rehearsed phrase seems sufficient for many people. That is what such people *want* to believe. It is convenient to forget that such accusations were levelled at the gatherings convened by John Wesley, General Booth and in the Hebrides revival, not to mention the Corinthian church in the NT!

It would be a good thing to check up on this in the situation of today and also to be precise about what we would count as being excessive. It is all too easy to forget what we want to forget; for instance, it is recorded in the Acts that on the day of Pentecost the man in the street thought that the 120 were drunk. No: that is not to advocate excess, but merely to try and make one think, in the living light of Calvary, exactly what is meant by 'excess'.

William Arthur, MA, writing in *The Tongue of Fire* published by the Wesleyan Methodist Book Room in 1894 writes:

> That bosom has yet to learn what is the feeling of moral sublimity, which has never been suddenly heaved with an emotion of uncontrollable adoration to God and the Lamb —an emotion which, though no voice told whence it came, by its movement in the depths of the soul further down than ordinary feelings reach, did indicate somehow that the touch of the Creator was traceable in it. They only who have felt such unearthly joy need attempt to conceive the outburst of that burning moment. Body, soul and spirit, glowing with one celestial fire would blend and pour out their powers in a rapturous 'Glory be to God'.

Again, Dr Martyn Lloyd-Jones in *Joy Unspeakable* has

this to say:

> Take your New Testament as it is. Look at the New Testament Christian, look at the New Testament church, and you see it vibrant with a spiritual life, and, of course, it is always life that tends to lead to excesses. *There is no problem of discipline in a graveyard* [the italics are mine]. There is no problem very much in a formal church. The problems arise when there is life. A poor sickly child is not difficult to handle, but when that child is well and full of life and of vigour, well, then you have your problems . . . and the problems of the early church were spiritual problems, problems arising because of the danger of going to excess in the spiritual realm.

One cannot help wondering if those claiming to be against excess, who have only taken for granted and never checked up on the accusation, know anything of such 'emotions of uncontrollable adoration'.

Two further points before we leave this question of excess. Most evangelicals feel that our Roman Catholic friends have carried the sacrament of the Lord's supper to excess in changing it into a mass. But that is never used as an argument for not remembering the Lord's death around the table. Others have gone to excess in their teaching about the second coming; but that is no reason for the rest of us to play the whole doctrine down.

Secondly, it is difficult to see why believers in 'the Word' should allow this one whispered word 'excess' to nullify the testimony of the New Testament on the matter. Which leads us to the second reason why some ask the question, 'Do I *have* to speak in tongues?'

Alibi teaching

By this I mean teaching that gives one a safe way out of a difficult spot (difficult, that is, to the status quo). In this case it is the teaching that 'tongues' ceased with the first century. Again let us hear Dr Lloyd-Jones:

> Go to 1 Corinthians 14 and there you find the type of meeting they had in the early church—'One hath a psalm, one hath a testimony, one hath an experience, one hath a tongue'—and so on. The whole thing was alive with a pneumatic spiritual power; and 'spiritual songs' means 'songs in the spirit'. The apostle says, 'I will pray with the spirit, and I will pray with the understanding also: I will sing with the spirit, and I will sing with the understanding also'. It is a type of singing about which the majority of us know nothing at all. So be careful lest you reduce even what was the normal regular life of the early Christian church down to the level of what has become customary in our churches.

Satanic insinuations

Under this heading we consider the most important reason why so many people, for so long have asked, 'Do I *have* to speak in tongues?' or have maintained an attitude even more hostile to the glossolalia. Jesus promised, 'Ye shall receive the power of the Holy Spirit coming upon you.' This indeed is the essence of the experience of the baptism with the Holy Spirit, and it is this power which Satan fears most of all. It is this power which upsets his kingdom, this power which convicts his followers of sin to the point of crying out 'What must I do to be saved?' It is this power that heals those who are oppressed of the devil, which enables men and women to follow in the footsteps of Jesus who went about doing good. This is the power which produces signs and wonders which witness that Jesus is alive and both Lord and Christ.

Undoubtedly the main reason why the modern church does not turn the modern world upside down is the absence of this power which comes when the baptism with the Holy Spirit is received *in its reality and fullness,* and which is not to be confused with merely speaking in tongues.

But, speaking in tongues, as we shall show later, is at least associated with such an infilling; and therefore if Satan can whisper this faith-destroying catch phrase into as many ears as possible, he limits the number of Christians who will seek such enduement with power.

Spurious manifestations

Satan also works on the basis of, 'If you can't beat them, join them.' In everything from the beginning he has always tried to get as near as possible to the activities of the living God (c.f. healing and necromancy).

It is well known that certain African tribes can be worked up into a demonic frenzy—aided and abetted by continuous 'beat' music, which music we have incorporated into our modern youth culture, and which I am sure, has opened the door to a much increased activity of demonic power in our modern society.

It is also sadly true that tongues can be so debased in practice by unsanctified Christians who almost get to learn their tongue by memory that it is denuded of all its power and significance. Recently I received a letter from someone in Lancashire who was 'over the moon' because we had prayed for him to have a 'new' tongue, in place of his old stereotyped one, and he had received just that. That is renewal.

To draw to a conclusion, 'Do I *have* to speak in tongues?' No, certainly not. It is not necessary to be regenerate, to live a clean sanctified Christian life, to have the Holy Spirit and know his guidance and illumination upon God's word and the evidence of the fruit of the Spirit in one's life.

No, you don't have to. But if you want the normal

NT experience of the baptism with the Spirit, then the answer has to be yes. If you would satisfy the longing of the great apostle, speaking under inspiration, 'I would that ye all speak with tongues' yes. If you would pray with the spirit, sing with the spirit yes. But again, I would emphasize that it seems to me that the whole idea of the question is wrong. Surely our attitude should be that if speaking in tongues is in the New Testament, if it is associated with the promise of the Father, the coming of the Holy Spirit for the endue-ment with power from on high, if it was the experience of Peter and Paul, the 120 and the first Gentile Chris-tians (to say the least) then we should desire such an experience with faith, anticipation and with all our heart and soul.

Tongues themselves are important, as we hope to show; but we may add that they are not of *major* im-portance, *unless they are resisted or refused.* Then they assume undue importance. This can be illustrated by a rather absurd parallel. Imagine a modern motorist who has just got a lovely new car. The engine is powerful and shines like a new pin. Oil is sticky messy stuff and he insists that he is not going to have any of it in his lovely new engine. Obviously, oil is important to the purpose of a car, namely to take one in comfort and with speed from A to B; but no sensible person would say, 'Come and see the oil in my new car.' So long as the oil is there, doing its job, nobody talks about it; but if for some stupid reason it is refused then trouble ensues.

Before we finally leave this somewhat odious ques-tion, let us take a quick look at the evidence of the Acts of the Apostles on the subject. This has been well docu-mented many times and a quick look will suffice.

In chapters 2, 10 and 19 the evidence of tongues is

specifically mentioned. In Acts 10:46 the word 'for' is used as direct proof of the fact that these Gentiles had received the outpoured Spirit not only *as well as* the original 120, but also *in the same manner* as those on the day of Pentecost.

The two occasions when no direct reference to tongues is made at the time of being baptized with the Spirit (Acts 8:17; 9:17) refer to the cases of the converts in Samaria after Philip's preaching and that of Saul of Tarsus, as he then was.

Paul specifically states later that he speaks in tongues more than the Corinthians (which would appear to be quite a lot!). This leaves the people of Samaria. Here it does not state that they spoke with tongues, but it does say two things that together are strong circumstantial evidence. First it says, in passing, that 'as yet he was fallen upon none of them'. If this experience is without manifestations, then we may ask, how did they know that he had fallen upon none of them? Secondly, the chapter records that when the apostles laid hands on people Simon the sorcerer witnessed something that he was willing to pay cash for as an addition to his stock-in-trade as one who regularly put on a show in the town. Presumably it must have been something external and unusual, and in view of all the other occasions in the Acts when the usual was speaking in other tongues, it seems reasonable to assume that it was the same in Samaria.

The record of the New Testament is in the last resort the only conclusive evidence for anything, but it is not out of place to mention the testimony of many millions of Christians of all denominations who today exercise this ministry and treasure it.

Why speak in tongues?

It seems so pointless; so strange to human logic. Why speak what to the hearers is utter nonsense when one could be using one's own language? It is not like the God of order and beauty whom we see in nature and the Bible. It is a fair question. Let us seek the answer.

First a general observation. God says, 'For my thoughts are not your thoughts, neither are your ways my ways' (Is 55:8). There are many strange things in Scripture. Paul speaks of one, for instance in Romans 9: why should God, desirous of getting his people out of Egypt, harden Pharaoh's heart to keep them in? The Scripture's own answer to this question is 'Nay but, O man, who art thou that repliest against God? Shall the thing formed say to him that formed it, Why hast thou made me thus? (Rom 9:20).

God has put glossolalia in the NT. We commonly agree that the preaching of the cross is to them that perish foolishness. Could it be that some Christians are carrying over into their spiritual appraisal of glossolalia some of the wisdom of the wise, by which wisdom the world knew not God and crucified the Lord of glory? The foolishness of God is wiser than men. The potter has ordained that the clay shall speak in tongues; what if the purpose is that, 'he might make known the riches of his glory on the vessels of mercy, which he had afore prepared unto glory, even us . . .'?

So, it is strange to the human mind. Agreed. But it is in the NT. So let us see what the NT has to say about its purpose.

A new prayer language

'He that speaketh in a tongue speaketh not unto men, but unto God' (1 Cor 14:2). Speaking to God is the simple definition of prayer. To commune with God, to make our requests known, to give thanks for and make mention of our friends and members of the body of Christ in general, as well as to worship in spirit and in truth are all most sensible and desirous things for any Christian to do. Speaking in tongues enables us in so doing to bypass the limitations of the human mind, unsanctified, alas, as it often is in so many traditional thought patterns still there from days when we walked according to the course of this world.

Which of us is not pretty regularly dogged with wandering thoughts during our private devotions? How wonderful of the Lord to give us a bypass into the realms of the Spirit.

A new praise and worship language

Jesus said that the Holy Spirit would 'glorify me: for he shall receive of mine, and shall show it unto you' (Jn 16:14). The apostle prays for the Ephesian saints that they may receive 'the spirit of wisdom and revelation in the knowledge of him: the eyes of your understanding being enlightened . . .' (Eph 1:17–18). It is only when we really *know* (not the same thing as 'knowing about') the Lord Jesus *by revelation* that we really get lost in wonder, love and praise. It is then that we find the limitations of our normal language quite insufficient. It is then, as we 'speak to God in mysteries', as we bypass our human limitations of thought and eradicate our unbelief in the process, as we sing and pray with the Spirit, as we bless and give thanks to God, it is then of all times that we may expect that we shall be 'changed into the same image from glory to glory, *even as by the Spirit of the Lord*' (2 Cor 3:18).

A new way of edification

'He that speaketh in an unknown tongue edifieth himself' (1 Cor 14:4). To edify oneself is most essential, especially for some whose normal church is still unrenewed, and who therefore receive very little inspired teaching from God's word. Sermonettes produce Christianettes! This biblical way to be edified is undoubtedly better than endless sermon tasting from place to place wherever there happens to be a well-known preacher. It is harder on the flesh and requires more discipline; but it is much more effective—and glorious.

Symbolic teaching

So far we have noted three specific scriptural reasons why we should speak in tongues. In addition if we look at *the symbolism* of speaking in tongues we shall find much that is not only illuminating but also which gives very good reason for this (to the human mind) rather strange practice. Let us explore.

The Holy Spirit is referred to in the Scriptures as a seal. A seal is, *inter alia*, a hallmark; and one of the hallmarks of human personality is speech.

Rusty, my little dog is intelligent; he is possessed of emotions; he appreciates warmth and cleanliness; he has memory and to a large extent understands what we say to him; sometimes, as we say, he is almost human. But for all that, I never expect him to speak to me! Speech belongs to man alone. So when the Holy Spirit clothes himself with human personality, God has ordained that he will first take possession of this unique faculty of self-expression.

Some men are highly intelligent, some are backward, but they have the faculty of speech. Whether men discuss abstract science and advanced technology or merely talk about today's dinner or baby's latest tooth, they all speak. Speech is common to all men; speech is a distinguishing mark of human personality.

For men to speak as the Holy Spirit gives them utterance is a fitting symbol, therefore, to signify that divine treasure has come to take control of earthen vessels.

'Death and life are in the power of the tongue' said the wise man (Prov 18:21). To a large extent it was the power of the tongue, with devilish oratory, by which Hitler lifted a nation from defeat and shame (after the treaty of Versailles) to proud and cruel arrogance and almost to world dominion.

At the other extreme, in the first century, by the foolishness of preaching a handful of men stood before potentates, brought confusion to sanhedrins, stilled the rabble, instructed the learned, preached the acceptable year of the Lord to the heathen and inflamed the hearts of ordinary folk to crusade for Christ in the face of imprisonment and torture—who, in short, turned the world upside down. Tongues of fire indeed! Divine fire possessing human speech (not speaking in tongues).

Speech is common to all nations. Divine inspiration is common to all glossolalia; but the languages differ. The tongue of fire was to spread from Jerusalem to Samaria and to the uttermost parts of the world. The same principle; the same symbolism; both ideally adapted to every man whatever his native tongue.

Not only is speech the hallmark of human personality, but the tongue is also the 'unruly member' which, says James, though little yet 'boasteth great things. Behold, how great a matter a little fire kindleth! And the tongue is a fire, a world of iniquity: so is the tongue among our members, that it defileth the whole body, and setteth on fire the course of nature; and it is set on fire of hell . . . the tongue can no man tame; it is an unruly evil, full of deadly poison' (Jas 3:5–8).

What a member! Capable of untold good and infinite evil—but uncontrollable. So God speaks through the symbolism and insists that he can and will control the uncontrollable, and tame the untameable; and consecrate only for good that which hitherto has been set on fire of hell.

How we should rejoice that the tongue of fire descended from the giver of speech, not only to change the nature of its source but of its destiny as well; the people at Pentecost were able to exclaim, 'we do hear them speak in our tongues the wonderful works of God' (Acts 2:11).

It has been fashionable for preachers to play down speaking in tongues because it is at the end of the list of the gifts; but there is no justification for this as comparison with other lists will show. Also, without divine love they are only sounding brass and tinkling cymbals. Here again, prejudiced men have been unfair to the glossolalia, for with equal logic one could minimize the value of prophecy, of understanding all mysteries and knowledge and faith. But there would be no sense in that; and neither is there any sense in minimizing tongues. Rather let us lay hold of the positive; what manner of person can I be if I have both divine love and the ability to speak with the tongues of men and of angels! Better to be a symbol than a cymbal!

There is still more hidden in the symbolism of speech. James says that speech is neither good nor bad —by it we can bless God or curse men. It is what Paul in Romans 6 calls a 'member' and as such it is to be yielded as an instrument. It all depends on who it is yielded to, who controls it (see Rom 6:13). This opens the way for us to consider the fundamental nature not only of speaking in tongues but also of all the gifts of the Spirit and to show how tongues holds the symbolism for them all. Speaking in tongues is an ideal symbol of the 'communion of the Holy Spirit' (part of the grace, as we call it, see 2 Cor 13:14). The word 'communion' in the Greek carries with it the idea of partnership. James and John were 'partners' in the fishing business, they 'communed' together (Lk 5:10).

The partnership of the Holy Spirit

The Holy Spirit and I are in business together, the King's business. Do not start in business on your own, said Jesus; wait until I send you a partner. How does the partnership work? Are we to pool our ideas and sift the best? Are we to have 'division of labour', he doing some jobs and I the others? He taking the difficult tasks, leaving the simpler ones to me? Am I to look after the secular and he the sacred? Am I to take care of preaching and call his aid when it comes to praying for the sick? Or am I to ask his help in everything? No, not even this last suggestion.

How then does the partnership work? How does it work in the matter of the glossolalia? That is a perfect symbol and exact illustration.

When I speak in tongues I yield a member of my human body, my tongue, to the control of the Holy Spirit; and then under his direction I do the speaking. You see, I have the ability to speak; the Spirit, being spirit has no such ability, but he has the ability to understand any language of men or angels, whereas I cannot do that. So we get together, he gives me the words and I do the speaking. The Spirit does not *help* me, he takes control of me to *use* me.

This is exactly how all the gifts work. Take healing for example. I have no power to heal, neither have the elders of a local church; but the Holy Spirit has boundless power to heal, but he has no hands to lay on the fevered brow, or to take the anointing oil and pour it on the patient's head. But I and the elders have hands. So I yield myself to his control and guidance to lay hands on the sick; the elders yield their voices to pray the prayer of faith and anoint with oil, and the Lord the Spirit causes the sick to recover, raising them up to health and strength.

This symbolism also teaches us that it is a partnership and not a dictatorship. That is why it is quite wrong for tongues to be called 'ecstatic utterance'. One is never lifted out of one's senses, never in a state of trance.

There are exceptional spiritual experiences of being caught up to the third heaven, whether in the body or out of the body being doubtful (2 Cor 12:2) but such experiences are outside the scope of this present enquiry and certainly do not refer to the normal glossolalia.

Some apparently 'go under the power' when receiving the infilling of the Spirit, but there is little evidence in the NT, if any, for this kind of thing *as related to being baptized with the Holy Spirit.* One cannot help feeling that this kind of manifestation is induced psychologically by some men, sincere enough in their motives, but liking, nevertheless a touch of the sensational to boost their advertising matter!

In times of revival there have been those, often in considerable numbers, who have been prostrated under the power of God. This, however, has more to do with the conviction of sin (a major ministry of the Holy Spirit) than the infilling of the Holy Ghost. At other times it has to do with satanic reaction to the power of God's Spirit in the individual concerned.

No. The whole concept of being baptized with the

Spirit is not a trance operation, but a conscious partnership where I yield my every member to the control of the Holy Spirit; and he takes one of these, initially the tongue, as a sign that the partnership has begun.

Basically, speaking in tongues is like prophecy in an unknown language. In nature the two are almost identical. Prophecy is defined in Deuteronomy 18:18: 'I will . . . put my words in his mouth'; and Peter's definition is: 'holy men of God spake as they were moved by the Holy Ghost' (2 Pet 1:21).

In the matter of prophecy Paul lays down a fundamental principle when he writes: 'the spirits of the prophets are subject to the prophets' (1 Cor 14:32). Here again the whole concept is that of a voluntary partnership; the prophet has his part to play in a conscious and sensible manner.

Paul speaks in the same context of one 'holding his peace' under certain circumstances. Of speaking by the gift of tongues he says that if there are no interpreters, 'let him keep silence in the church'. This he could not do under trance conditions. The seance is the counterfeit. Satan is the author of this; he does take men captive at his will. Not so the Holy Spirit. The language of the Spirit is this: 'I beseech you therefore, brethren, by the mercies of God, that ye present (same root word as "yield") your bodies a living sacrifice, holy, acceptable unto God, which is your reasonable service (or spiritual worship)'!

In this connection we may say that glossolalia is a kind of sacrament: it is an outward sign of an inward reality. The outward sign, of course, is the speaking in tongues. The inner reality is that I have yielded my will to the Holy Spirit, I have given him full permission to use any of my human faculties.

One further word is used in Scripture in relation to

the Holy Spirit; the word 'earnest': 'the earnest of the Spirit' (2 Cor 1:22). In the Ephesian letter Paul uses the same phrase with the idea that the coming of the Holy Spirit is only a foretaste of the fullness of our inheritance which we shall know at the day of rapture.

The modern equivalent of 'earnest' is a down-payment. One pays a deposit now and receives the goods, on the understanding that future instalments will be paid regularly.

In this light we may view glossolalia as the earnest of the Spirit, i.e. the Spirit's down-payment. As I willingly yield to the Spirit's possession, he takes and uses one member, the tongue, on a kind of down-payment basis, on the understanding that further instalments of this dual operation will be forthcoming.

These instalments will be forthcoming at all times when I need his ability—and if I only knew it and would acknowledge it, that is at all times!—and also in relation to all other of my faculties and members.

At the down-payment he takes and uses my tongue. In later instalments he will take and use my hands, my feet, my eyes, my ears, my mind, my compassion . . . in short, any and every faculty of soul and body. Any of these, at any time.

Corporate worship

Speaking in tongues (as distinct from the gift) for the individual, as we have insisted, is always for *private* use. There is one exception to this rule, however, namely its use in corporate worship.

Paul speaks of 'singing with the spirit' (1 Cor 14:15). Now, singing is something we normally do together in public; and to sing together 'with the Spirit' is not only permissible but very blessed. None of the objections against speaking in tongues in public are valid when we sing together with the Spirit. The others do not understand my singing in tongues; but I am not singing *to* them but *with* them in worship to God.

If they have to listen to me speaking in tongues alone in public they are not edified (which is why the apostle insists that I should not do it) but when we all sing together we are all edified together.

In passing, it is well to notice that this is 'singing *with* the Spirit' (I prefer the capital 'S' throughout, though there is no such distinction in Greek, so I am told) and not 'singing *in* the Spirit'. All prayer and supplication (and singing), whether with the Spirit or with the understanding, whether in English or in tongues, is to be '*in* the Spirit' (Eph 6:18).

I used to know a lady (she is with the Lord now), the widow of a Strict Baptist minister. She was elderly, a cultured, delightful and sanctified Christian. She used to tell of a dream she had had years before the days of renewal. In this dream she went to heaven; and one of the things she remembered most vividly was what she called the angelic singing. Many years later, the first time she heard corporate worship with the Spirit at a conference in Devon, she told us that what she had just heard was as near as was humanly possible to what she had heard in her dream.

Usually in this corporate worship 'with the Spirit' the Holy Spirit seems to direct the tune as well as give the words. The result is an unconscious harmony that is quite beautiful. This is a kind of double partnership. At other times a leader may be prompted to ask the people to continue singing the tune of a hymn or chorus but use the words of the Spirit. This too is very inspiring. Again it is a kind of double partnership: we provide the voice and the tune and the Holy Spirit the words. This corporate worship is much the best when it is entirely spontaneous, when the whole gathering of people are flowing together in the Spirit, responding corporately to his promptings. The singing starts spontaneously and remarkably, for no apparent reason, draws to a close spontaneously—all together. It is all very beautiful and inspiring.

Some seem to think that Paul plays all this down in 1 Corinthians 14 (though I do not agree at all). Others think this is the very acme of divine worship (as I do). Both points of view have some backing in the chapter. Let each assembly be fully persuaded in its own leadership and teaching, be fully led by the Spirit and be anxious that everything will be done to edification and done decently and in order.

We must now turn our attention to the actual 'gift of tongues' as it is to be used publicly with the twin gift of interpretation.

Interpretation

This gift is always associated with the twin gift of interpretation, so much so that the apostle insists that if there is no interpreter present in the church, then it should not be exercised.

As we have written before, the gift of tongues is for public use, and as such is given to the body of Christ; and its use in little private fellowship times amongst friends—whilst acknowledging that in the last resort (a point strongly emphasized by the Plymouth Brethren) such gatherings *can* be called meetings of the 'church'—is, I think suspect and not to be encouraged. Why? Chiefly because the 'others', especially the leadership, are not there to 'judge'. Incidentally, to 'judge' in the NT means 'to weigh in the balance' and does not mean to condemn.

In practice today charismatic renewal people have followed the mainline Pentecostals before them and made these twin gifts virtually the same as prophecy— at one remove, so to speak. That is, the interpretation is given as the Lord speaking a message to his people.

I personally think this is a pity and a mistake. What often happens, I think, is that the so-called interpretation is actually a prophecy which has been held back, but then the tongue which needs an interpretation has galvanized the person into giving his/her prophecy.

Preferably, we should take 1 Corinthians 14:2 as applicable here: 'he that speaketh in an unknown tongue speaketh not unto men, but unto God'; in which case the interpretation should not be addressed to the church as prophecy, but to God. That is, it will be either prayer or praise and worship.

One may say that if the interpretation is of the Spirit, then he knows what it should be, without our laying down guide-lines as to its direction. Such reasoning, however, overlooks two important factors: (1) The Holy Spirit never moves contrary to the Scriptures, and (2) As the spirits of the prophets are subject to the prophets, so equally are the spirits of the interpreters. So, if one kind of usage is accepted as normal and correct, then the interpreters will fit into that pattern— even if it is not according to the mind of the Spirit.

Many a time I have been in a service where praise and worship was flowing beautifully, with a lovely sense of the Lord's presence; and there has come a tongue with the traditional form of interpretation, and when that was over the whole meeting has gone quite flat, with little or no sense of the Lord's presence any more. Whereas, if the interpretation had been the Spirit's ministry of magnifying the Lord Jesus, helping our infirmities, then we would have been lifted even higher into heavenly places. This is very common and very sad. The only justification of our current practice could be drawn from 1 Corinthians 14:6: 'Now, brethren, if I come unto you speaking with tongues, what shall I profit you, *except* I shall speak to you either by revelation, or by knowledge, or by prophesying, or by doctrine?'

But it is far from clear as to whether this can be regarded as justification or not. It *could* mean that the interpretation of the tongue is either a revelation or a prophecy or a doctrine; but it seems far more logical to assume that these are four *alternatives* to tongues and not a possible *use* of tongues.

At the moment these twin gifts are more popularly used than any other of the gifts of the Spirit. One cannot help wishing and praying that the spiritual standard of their current use could be very considerably raised. There is tremendous potential in the Spirit's ability to lift our times of praise and worship to altogether new heights of glory through the proper exercise of these gifts. I pray these few remarks may be used to this end.

The benefits of speaking in tongues

I hesitate to write of things I cannot substantiate from the New Testament, but it is undoubtedly true that speaking in tongues has therapeutic value; it relieves the stress and tension which plague so many lives today. Indeed, some Christians' lives are tense and stressful simply, or chiefly, because they do not speak in tongues.

To neglect or refuse to speak in tongues is like putting an artificial dam across a fast-flowing stream. Pressure builds up, and that is stress; and sometimes the whole build-up overflows into the surrounding territory of one's personality, tending towards all kinds of psychosomatic troubles. To release the dam is therapeutic indeed.

To hold back in tongues (or any other gift) undoubtedly *grieves* the Holy Spirit, because it quenches his ministry and questions his Lordship. Therefore if I hold back, the result is not only stress in the soul but poverty in the spiritual life also.

In addition, there is a positive side to this matter. Speaking in tongues in general is a healthful occupation. In the perpetual mad rat-race of modern existence there are many Christians who sadly have to resort to taking pills as a normal routine: some take pep pills to get going and others sleeping pills to slow down and some need both! To all such I commend the practice of speaking in tongues as an effective alternative.

Some find it easier to sing in tongues than to speak. If so, then by all means sing! Some, also, when seeking to 'begin' for the first time find it easier to over-leap the self-conscious barrier by joining in corporate worship with the Spirit (i.e. singing in tongues). Our great high priest is touched with the feelings of our infirmities and bids us draw near to the throne of grace without fear; so if singing with everybody else eases you into this spiritual exercise, then just sing. Speaking will follow in due course.

Tongues and tongues . . .

In this chapter I have made a suggestion that the interpretation of tongues should be directed Godward, namely, in praise and worship addressed to our Lord; it should not be prophecy at one remove, so to speak, namely a message through the Spirit to the church. This I consider to be the most important thing I have to say on the subject of interpretation.

There are other things that perhaps need clarification however. The first of which is that this gift is the gift of *interpretation* and not *translation*. Elsewhere we have also insisted that this ministry has nothing to do with linguistic ability; it is an interpretation by the Holy Spirit of the content of the message in tongues. This explains something that often puzzles people who are unfamiliar with these things, namely, that sometimes the interpretation is either much longer or shorter than the original tongue. This could also be the case if it were a translation say from Latin into English; but this has no relevance because it is not a translation, but an interpretation (cf. Dan 5:1–28).

Sometimes the tongue is in a known language as on the day of Pentecost, but it does not have to be a known language; though when one considers how many different languages and dialects there are in the whole world this presents no problem. But the New Testament does speak of tongues of men *and of angels* so there is no problem here either. Someone has said in this connection that the difference between the day of Pentecost, when there were Parthians, Medes, Elamites, etc—sixteen in all!—in the audience, and today is not in the tongues but in the audience. A valid remark—but not frightfully important.

In the early 1960s at a well known mid-day prayer meeting for business people in the City held at St Bride's Church, Fleet Street, on one occasion there was a tongue and after the service a man in long orthodox flowing robes approached the leader and asked who it was that had spoken with such fluency and correctness in a little known old Greek language. I once spoke in a tongue in Philadelphia, USA and some thought it was a variation of Yiddish; and there have been recorded stories of missionaries about to be killed by hostile natives speaking in the local vernacular, and thus not only saving their own lives but also causing the tribe to turn to Christ. I cannot vouch for the authority of such stories but in any case, such occurrences are outside the normal scope and purpose of these twin gifts.

I have known quite a few cases where the interpretation has been a special message from the Lord to the actual person doing the interpreting. When this is perceived by someone in leadership or someone with the gift of discerning of spirits and then hands are laid on the interpreter in question to confirm the message great blessing in many ways has been the outcome.

Occasionally there are problems in a public church meeting in relation to tongues and interpretation:
(1) If the tongue is definitely not of the right spirit.
(2) If the tongue was innocuous, but not at an appropriate time.
(3) If the tongue is deemed to be in order but there is no interpretation forthcoming—only a deadly prolonged silence.

What should the leader do in such circumstances? There is no hard and fast rule; rather each case must be dealt with on its own merits and the leader can expect clear guidance from the Holy Spirit, especially from a word of wisdom or a word of knowledge either through himself or another. Very often the best thing to do, after a short wait is to proceed with the service, either with or without a very brief word saying that the tongue was inappropriate, or that it was a tongue of praise from the person who gave the word and that we should now proceed.

If, on the other hand, the tongue was from an evil spirit then it is wise to proceed with the service in the best possible way, and then speak to the person who gave the spurious tongue after the service, either forbidding any repetition of such a tongue or preferably with a ministry of deliverance from the evil spirit, leading to a filling with the Holy Spirit.

Only if such wrong tongues, of whatever sort, persist should the matter be dealt with publicly by the leader. I did this once in Devon years ago and after the service a group of mature leaders came to me to thank me, saying they had been waiting for a long time for someone to do just that!

7
Healing

'Now there is at Jerusalem by the sheep market a pool, which is called in the Hebrew tongue Bethesda, having five porches' (Jn 5:2). The pool called Bethesda in Jerusalem was a permanent site of healing. At the pool there were five porches, five porticos where the sick, the impotent, the blind, the lame and the withered lay waiting for the moment of healing—waiting and hoping. One man had been waiting a lifetime, thirty-eight years.

There are five different 'porticos' of healing in the New Testament. Five different ministries: laying on of hands; anointing with oil; praying for one another; the word of authority; the gifts of healing. We will look briefly at each of these. But first let us make a few contrasts between conditions long ago in Bethesda and today.

Bethesda was in Jerusalem. There was only one Bethesda. If you were not able to get to Bethesda and stay there it was just too bad. Today the healing Christ is not confined to any one place or time. He is the healing Lord, and wherever two or three are gathered together in his name there he is in the midst of them.

Some find the holy communion table a special place of healing, and so it is, but it is not an 'only' place. I have known people healed at the back of the church as everybody was leaving the service; and Edgar Trout laid hands on someone in the street in the centre of Bradford and the Lord healed. In church or hospital, at home or abroad, it makes no difference.

Bethesda means 'house of mercy' and as we sing today, 'his mercy flows on like a river, his love is unmeasured and free; his grace is forever sufficient'; he can heal anywhere, any time.

The healing venue was a pool. This was stagnant water disturbed only occasionally by a visiting angel.

In Christ, water is always 'living', it is a fountain, it is springing up into life of all kinds, bringing wholeness to the whole man—which is the best definition of Christ's healing ministry. The ministry of healing in the church, which is the body of Christ, is to express the mercy of the one whose unchanging name is Jehovah Rapha—'I am the Lord that healeth thee'.

After the disturbing of the water at Bethesda it was only the first into the pool who received healing. I often think of this when ministering to a long queue of people at the front of a church and after a while remind the people that there is as much of the Saviour's compassion and healing virtue at the end of the queue as at the front!

The man at the pool whom Jesus asked if he would like to be made whole replied, 'Sir, I have no man, when the water is troubled, to put me into the pool'. In his weakness he was dependent on man's help even to get to the source of his potential healing. Today God uses men as his instruments but they are by no means

essential; and in any case it is not man's aid that the sick
are in need of. When the disciples could not handle the
situation Jesus said: 'Bring him to me'. None now need
help even to get to the Saviour. Anyone can draw near
in full assurance of faith to a throne of grace without
any human intercessor.

Finally, exciting as it must be to see an angel (I never
have!), we are looking to the one who has been 'made
so much better than angels'. Amazing grace, wonderful
Lord, all powerful name. Now to look at each of the
five porticos:

Laying on of hands

> He laid his hands upon a few sick folk, and healed them
> (Mk 6:5); these signs shall follow them that believe; In my
> name . . . they shall lay hands on the sick, and they shall
> recover (Mk 16:17–18).

As mentioned elsewhere, there is in the charismatic
renewal movement a special emphasis on the ministry
of the laying on of hands, and as a result this is the most
usual ministry of healing in our day.

Laying on of hands is a means of identification with
the sufferer, an expression of the compassion of the
Lord. He was regularly 'moved with compassion' whilst
on earth in the flesh and he is still the same. When the
woman touched the hem of his garment, he insisted
that virtue had gone out of him and he was aware of it.
By faith we can be 'filled with all the fulness of God'
and the laying on of hands is a means whereby that
indwelling virtue of Christ can be communicated in the
name of Jesus. Sometimes one is aware of this outgoing
virtue, but more often than not one is entirely unaware
of it. But the awareness is not important in any case;
what is important is our being open, free and sanctified

channels, moving in simple faith according to the Scriptures.

Similarly, sometimes the patient feels an unusual warmth or something like a small electric shock going through him at the time of the laying on of hands; sometimes under some ministries people fall to the ground 'slain under the power' as they claim. But all these cases of different reactions are quite unimportant. Faith alone matters in the last resort.

Anointing with oil; praying for one another

> Is any sick among you? let him call for the elders of the church; and let them pray over him, anointing him with oil in the name of the Lord . . . Confess your faults one to another, and pray one for another, that ye may be healed (Jas 5:14, 16).

I have put these two together under one heading for two reasons: first, they are both to be found in James 5 and, second, because they are both set in the context of the church: 'Is any sick *among you*?' Together these two should be the normal reaction of any local church to sickness in their midst. A few points need special mention.

The initiative should come from the sick person. 'Is any sick among you? let him call for the elders of the church . . .' This therefore, should be the first thing a Christian sick person should do. Unfortunately this is not usually the case; rather one's first instinct is to call for the doctor. One cannot speak too highly of the medical profession and the dedication and skill of the doctors; but what of the dedication of fellow Christians? Are they not equally dedicated?

We have to admit that as far as those who are in employment are concerned the position is complicated by the fact that the worker must have a doctor's chit to be off work and receive benefit, etc., but does this not also reveal where our first hopes lie, the object of our faith?

To a large extent however the Christian is absolved of this charge for the simple reason that he is not taught by his leaders what his first priority should be; and that for the obvious reason that often there are no elders in the church who are available to be 'called'. This is no quibble about who is an elder or what he is called in a modern church; rather it is a question of whether there are any who are willing and able to pray a prayer of faith for the sick. The question is whether there are any who have given themselves to such a ministry who are available on a regular basis.

An increasing number of churches are now holding a healing session say once a month, usually in conjunction with a service of holy communion. This is a step in the right direction and, in the context of recent tradition, is excellent.

Many Christians believe that Christ's healing ministry is exercised through the doctors. Certainly, in the last resort all medical skill is from God and it is only right that we should pray for God's wisdom and knowledge to be expressed through the doctor's ministrations in any particular case. Such prayers are often answered in a marvellous way. It is impossible and appalling to think of a world without medical skill and we cannot rate too highly the devotion and the amazing achievements of modern medicine and surgery—and we thank God accordingly.

But having said all that—and one feels that one has not said it well enough or sufficiently—I cannot see that the doctors fulfil the healing ministry expressed in James 5. If we could have more and more doctors who were expressly Christian, who openly tried to view their work as co-operating with God and the church, then the ideal would be for such a partnership in the healing ministry amongst the Lord's people.

One final point: it is essential to notice that it is the prayer of faith that heals the sick in conjunction with anointing with oil. This lays the onus directly on the shoulders of the elders. It is their faith and not that of the sick person that is the saving factor. I say it is essential to notice this, because in cases where no healing results it is so easy for the sufferer to be plunged into further distress by the thought that they did not have faith. And it can be disastrous when, under such conditions, it is implied that it is their fault they are not healed. This is a cruel accusation and wholly wrong and unfounded.

But to leave the matter there merely shifts the blame, the 'cruel accusation', on to the shoulders of the elders. It may well rest there, but as we indicate in the chapter on the problems in the healing ministry, there are so many factors which relate to whether a person is healed or not that it is quite unfair to stigmatize the elders with all the blame and responsibility. We should undoubtedly witness much more healing in the body of Christ if instead of blaming the elders (and others) we gave ourselves to fervent prayer on their behalf in general, and in particular for this special aspect of their ministry.

The word of authority

> Then Peter said, Silver and gold have I none; but such as I have give I thee: In the name of Jesus Christ of Nazareth rise up and walk (Acts 3:6).

This incident is in fulfilment of Jesus' promise of faith in Mark 11 where he said, '. . . he shall have whatsoever he saith'. There is no church setting here, or any request for healing or offering up of prayer. It is a combination of the exercise of the gift of miracles and the gift of faith, both of which we shall be looking at later.

This same ministry was exercised by Peter when he said to Aeneas: 'Jesus Christ maketh thee whole: arise, and make thy bed.' Paul used it at Lystra when he said to a man in his congregation who was impotent in his feet and who had been a cripple since his birth—and who, when he heard Paul speaking, found faith rising in his heart to such an extent that Paul recognized that he had faith to be healed—'Stand upright on thy feet.' And it is reported that 'he leaped and walked'.

The gifts of healing

This gift alone among the nine mentioned in 1 Corinthians 12, is in the plural, which may be to emphasize the many and varied kinds of gifts in this sphere of ministry.

There is also a plurality of interpretations of this gift. Some hold that the one who receives the gift is the sick person. This, of course, is true in a way, but is rather a naïve thought. Others hold that one person receives this gift and henceforth goes on to be used especially in the healing ministry. Others yet again—and I among them—feel that any Spirit-filled Christian may draw upon the grace of the Lord and claim the operation of this gift in any particular situation.

Certainly if the gift is in operation then one moves in unflinching faith and sees the healing accomplished. Maybe the plurality indicates that all of these views can be correct if exercised in real faith in differing circumstances.

Following our main theme that the gifts of the Spirit

are tools for the job, surely the main job to be done is that of outreach. This gift of healing, more than any other, was the key to much of the huge success of the apostles and evangelists of the early church. When Philip went down to the city of Samaria and preached Christ to them it is reported (Acts 8:6–7), 'the people with one accord gave heed unto those things which Philip spake, hearing and seeing the miracles which he did. For unclean spirits, crying with loud voice, came out of many that were possessed with them: and many taken with palsies, and that were lame, were healed.'

Similarly, when Paul was shipwrecked on the island of Melita, after he had prayed for Publius' father who was healed, he prayed with others who also had diseases in the island and they were healed. We are not told the upshot of this but I imagine it is very likely that a new local church was formed on the island.

One remembers with gratitude to God the early ministry of George Jeffries in this country some years ago. Wherever he went the crowds queued to hear him and it was his gift of healing that drew them. After a few weeks in any one place he usually left a live and large local church, drawn mostly from complete outsiders. We are sadly in need of such a ministry today. 'And they went forth, and preached every where, the Lord working with them, and confirming the word with signs following' (Mk 16:20).

Jehovah-Rophi: 'I am the Lord that healeth thee' (Ex 15:26)

The first mention in the Scriptures of any basic theme is I believe of great importance and usually lays a firm foundation for all subsequent teaching on the subject. Such is the case with healing.

Jehovah-Rophi is one of seven hyphenated Jehovah names found in the Old Testament. Bearing in mind Jesus' own identification with Jehovah, the one who is called I AM, we can safely view each one of these Jehovah names as underlining a major aspect of the life and ministry of our Lord Jesus Christ. It is in this connection that healing is brought into its proper place in the church's continuation of the ministry which Jesus 'began both to do and to teach'. We cannot accept Jehovah-Jireh, the Lord will provide; Jehovah-Nissi, the Lord my banner; Jehovah-Tsidkenu, the Lord my righteousness; Jehovah-Shalom, the Lord my peace; Jehovah-Shammah, the Lord is there; and Jehovah-Raah, the Lord my shepherd—we cannot accept these six and reject Jehovah-Rophi, I am the Lord that healeth thee.

So let us pursue the thought that the foundations of the Bible's teaching on healing are laid here in the first mention of the subject.

Before we look at the context, notice four very simple but fundamental things using a well-known preaching habit of taking each word in a sentence and emphasizing that particular word to bring out its important truth.

(1) *I am*. This is present, continuous; not I was, or will be, but (cf. Jesus himself, who said 'I am that I am') as the Lord told Moses to say to the Israelites: 'I AM hath sent me unto you' (Ex 3:14), this affirmation of his being the healing Saviour holds the continuous sense.

The healing ministry of Jesus is written large, very large, in the four gospels and each commission by our Lord to his disciples contained explicitly or implicitly a call to continue his healing ministry.

(2) I am *the Lord*. He is Lord—Lord over all the

powers and works of Satan. His name is above every other name. Your sickness has a name, whether a simple one or an unpronounceable medical name; whatever it is, the name of Jesus is above it! He is Lord.

When Jesus cried 'It is finished' he meant everything that was wrecked in the Garden had been redeemed.

When Jesus was asked once if he *could* help and heal, he answered that that was not the point—only whether the questioner could believe. 'All power', he finally said as he prepared to leave this earth, 'All power is given unto me in heaven *and in earth*' (Mt 28:18). He is Lord. God has put all things under his feet.

(3) I am the Lord *that healeth*. Here again just as the Lord is our peace, our righteousness, and our shepherd all the time, so he is the unchanging healing Saviour who keeps on healing.

(4) I am the Lord that healeth *you*. It is personal, though not to the exclusion of larger issues, for God's purpose is in the fullness of time to gather in one all things in Christ, both which are in heaven and which are on earth, even in him. But our concern at the moment is with personal healing. All the present continuous lordship of Jesus is available for you.

Now let us see what we have to learn from the context of this revelation of Jesus as healing Lord.

The water was bitter

This underlines the fact, obvious to all who are sick, that sickness is a bitterness. This refutes the pious suggestion that the sick ones are sharing the sufferings of Christ and should therefore be glad for such a privilege. (See the chapter on problems.)

The people murmured

It is easy to murmur; it is understandable if and when one is enduring the bitterness of sickness. It is easy and understandable but not a good thing to do. It says they murmured against Moses but in reality it was against God.

'God, God, why does this have to happen to me? . . . Don't you know what a good church-going Christian I am, how much I give in time and money, etc., etc.?' It looks a bit ridiculous in black and white print but it is a pretty common feeling and frequently expressed vehemently.

Murmuring against God is virtually blaming God for the sickness, whereas in almost every case it has nothing to do with God at all; but is merely the inevitable consequence of the fact that we live in a sinful world and each generation has to bear the cumulative build-up of evil things of all kinds including germs, viruses, bacteria and the like; plus the fact that most of us constantly ignore God's advice about healthy living, eating and drinking. Rather than murmur, we should emulate Moses and cry unto the Lord.

The Lord showed him a tree

This was Jehovah's reply to Moses when he cried to the Lord. This surely must typify the tree of which Peter speaks: 'Who his own self bare our sins in his own body on the tree . . . by whose stripes ye were healed' (1 Pet 2:24).

It is chiefly because of this passage (the first and fundamental) and a detailed study of Isaiah 53 and Matthew 8:17, which quotes Isaiah 53:4 in relation to Jesus healing all that were sick, that I personally am convinced that healing is in the atonement.

If the atonement reversed all the evil consequences of the fall, then that automatically puts healing there. But this is a controversial matter and I have no wish to be dogmatic on the point.

In any case it makes no difference to the reality of the healing ministry, as one can put all the healing in the world within any of the great promises of God available in response to an active faith.

The conditions

'If thou wilt diligently . . .' these are the usual terms of the old covenant, the conditions for blessing under law. In all matters when we use the OT to teach about the NT (and that is probably its chief present-day function) the only thing, apart from local details, that needs to be changed is this matter of the covenant. God, his purposes and his promises all remain the same, but the covenant has been changed since Calvary. Now it is always, for all things, a covenant of grace through faith. In the OT as here, it was 'if you do this, this and this'— and all of it—'and not do that and the other, then God will bless you; he will heal you'. In the NT we are 'saved', with all that that means, solely because of God's grace and our response of faith, 'without the deeds of the law' (Rom 3:28).

This is very important in relation to healing because a lot of people seem to think they have a claim on God for healing because of their good works. This is the curse of the law—and a huge curse it is!

To human logic there is a certain contradiction in this passage, but there is divine provision for God's people on a higher level than logic. The passage says 'I will put none of these diseases upon thee, which I have brought upon the Egyptians: for I am the Lord that healeth thee.' Now if we are not to have any diseases, we are never to be sick, and therefore we do not require a healing Lord!

This, I believe, prefigures God's provision for his people to enjoy good health. I would encourage a living faith for all to lay hold of our Lord's promise: 'I am come that they might have life, and that they might have it more abundantly' (Jn 10:10). I see no reason why this should not include abundant physical and mental health as well as spiritual life, particularly if we lay hold of God's provision in the apostle's teaching that we can be 'filled with all the fulness of God' (Eph 3:19).

I am sure there is no sickness in God's fullness. Quite simply: Christ is a whole man in every meaning of the word and he is our life! Hallelujah!

Receiving your healing

Before reading this section you should read Matthew 8:1–4.

There were multitudes milling around, but one person was special. Faith makes even a leper special. It was the same with the woman who touched the hem of his garment. Everybody was touching him but she was special. Why? Because of her faith.

The leper ought not to have been mingling amongst the crowd at all; he was unclean and to be ostracized. But faith overleaps all barriers to get to Jesus. Faith approaches not because of its rights but because of its need and its conviction that Jesus can if he will—and finds that he does will!

The leper came and he worshipped. No doubt in eastern fashion he literally fell on his face before the Lord. He had no theology and I doubt if he even thought of Jesus as the Messiah, but nevertheless he worshipped. There is no better place to receive your healing than the place and the time of worship. I remember praying for a partially blind lady in France early on in the service. Apparently nothing happened but the service proceeded and we worshipped the Lord in a hymn of praise and suddenly to our surprise the lady cried out 'I can see'. She held out her hymn book: 'I can read it' she said. We continued to worship—all the more so!

Although I doubt if the leper would know any theology about the lordship of Christ yet he worshipped saying 'Lord'. That, too, was special. He acknowledged Jesus as Lord not as a theological fact but in the context of his need. This is a simple lesson we need so much to learn in our day. If we are Anglicans, it is so easy to sing the *Te Deum* in general terms, and it is true of course; but really to worship and say 'Lord' in the context of our need, that is the place of faith.

The leper had doubts as to whether Jesus would be willing, not as to his ability. So often that too is our doubt. Jesus immediately quelled such doubts and fears: 'I will' he said and he touched him.

Touch is important. Ask any courting couple! Whether Jesus touches you, as in the case of the leper, or you touch Jesus, as for the woman, either way as you worship, reach out and touch the Lord.

Not discerning the Lord's body

> . . . not discerning the Lord's body. For this cause many are weak and sickly among you, and many sleep (1 Cor 11:29–30).

One Saturday night my friend and I were praying for quite a few sick people at the altar in a church in South

Wales. At the end only one lady was left at the altar. We had prayed for the healing of her eyes (she wore very thick-lensed glasses). It was obvious to us that we were getting nowhere. So Philip who has the gifts of the word of knowledge and discerning of spirits began to speak with the lady again. He asked about her home life. In confusion, she eventually acknowledged that relationships in the home were more like relationships between cats and dogs than those of a Christian family. We counselled her to go home and put this right and come to be prayed for again in the morning.

She went home repentant, put the matter right with her husband and family—and came to church on Sunday morning without her glasses!

The Lord's body

There are two ways in which the NT speaks of the Lord's body. First: Christ's literal physical body and second, the church which is his body.

This particular verse, set in the context of the holy communion service refers, I believe, to the Lord's body in both these applications.

Jesus' physical human body. Many remain weak and sickly 'among you' i.e. in the church, because they fail to discern that Jesus' body bore the stripes by which we are healed. They claim forgiveness and possibly much else from the cross of Calvary, they give (rightly) strong emphasis to the blood of Christ. In the holy communion they feed on the bread by faith in their hearts, but never seem to understand that it is 'by his stripes that we are healed' (1 Pet 2:24) and of course it was his body that bore the stripes.

All such should ask the Holy Spirit to open the eyes of their understanding to see Jesus in this way on the cross; or maybe even ask to be prayed with for release from a blockage concerning this spiritual revelation.

But this chapter is mainly to deal with the other aspect of the Lord's body.

The church which is his body. When the apostle writes that we fail to discern the Lord's body, in this context he means that we fail to realize the fundamental implications of what it means to be a member of Christ's mystical body.

When we fail to discern the Lord's body in this way we ignore the fact that we are members one of another in the body of Christ and either ignore or continue to violate the essential nature of the body which Paul spells out in some detail in both Romans 12 and 1 Corinthians 12—both chapters which deal with spiritual gifts.

Translated into this body metaphor, our attitudes appear completely ridiculous. For instance, how stupid for my nose to get the idea that it is superior to my ear, and therefore make all kinds of endeavour to displace the ear and do the job of hearing itself. Or for the eye to be jealous of the mouth; or for my left hand to resent my right hand because I am right-handed. If, for instance, I am doing some painting and decorating and I upset the paint can with my left hand; what does the right hand do? Turn to the left hand and call it all kinds of names and insist that it spilt the paint, therefore it must clean up the mess? How stupid and ridiculous, yet members of the body of Christ seem to do this sort of thing quite often!

The NT has some extremely strong things to say about such behaviour. Take James 3:14–16 for example: 'But if ye have bitter envying and strife in your hearts, glory not, and lie not against the truth. This wisdom descendeth not from above, but is earthly, sensual, devilish. For where envying and strife is, there is confusion and every evil work.' Not only envy and jealousy, but strife. How much of this have we seen in the body of Christ? There is less now between the different denominations, but often still plenty within any one denomination and often within one local church.

'Earthly, sensual, devilish. For where envying and strife is, there is confusion and every evil work' . . . not discerning the body of Christ—'for this cause many are weak and sickly among you'! These things, says the apostle, are 'in your hearts'; but we are supposed to have new hearts, clean hearts and Christ is our life; we have been made partakers of divine nature. But when Christ was reviled he reviled not again.

Or again, take the matter of forgiveness. How often do we hear the phrase: 'Yes, I've forgiven him/her, but I can't forget'—which means we don't really forgive at all. Jesus had strong words to say about this too, though I fear they are also constantly ignored. Take the most well-known instance of all, namely the Lord's prayer: 'Forgive us our trespasses *as we forgive them that trespass against us*.' Jesus said: 'Therefore I say unto you, what things soever ye desire, when ye pray, believe that ye receive them, and ye shall have them. And when ye stand praying, forgive, if ye have ought against any: that your Father also which is in heaven may forgive you your trespasses. But if ye do not forgive, neither will your Father which is in heaven forgive your trespasses' (Mk 11:24–26). I wonder how much we are forgiven if it is 'as we forgive' i.e. commensurate with *our* forgiving.

We insist that if it is not our fault then the other party must make the first move and do the forgiving. But

Jesus says: 'Therefore if thou bring thy gift to the altar, and there rememberest that *thy brother hath ought against thee*; leave there thy gift before the altar, and go thy way; first be reconciled to thy brother, and then come and offer thy gift' (Mt 5:23–24). It is in this context that in the holy communion service the apostle asks us to 'judge ourselves'.

In the early Fountain Trust conferences we used to say that the Lord was correcting our attitudes towards those from other denominations which we said had been rather like two hedgehogs trying to have fellowship!

How much better if we heed the apostle's final request as we break bread together: 'Wherefore, my brethren, when ye come together to eat, tarry one for another'. You may be surprised and delighted to find you are also healed.

8

Problems with Healing

There are mysteries connected with the ministry of
healing to which we do not know the answers. This
means we have problems. It is good that we face them
squarely and honestly.

Many years ago I remember going to hear Oral
Roberts preach in a football ground in South Wales. He
was being mightily used in healing in the USA at that
time. He began by saying that in the early days of his
ministry he felt he knew all the answers. Now the more
he went along the more he felt he had to learn. That is
true of us all. Nobody knows all the answers, so let us
take a hard look at the problems.

These days I have a personal problem in as much as
my wife is not fully healed even though a great many
Christians have prayed for her. At the end of 1976 Jean
had a very serious stroke. For a while she could neither
walk nor talk and she hung between life and death. She
actually managed to say to me in hospital: 'Dear, you
had better let me go.'

However we persisted in prayer and the laying on of

hands and finally with the help of brain surgery the Lord raised her up. I say she is a walking miracle! But she is not fully healed, and we don't know why. After we have done all we know how she has remained the same these last few years.

We are deeply grateful for her partial restoration but I live with a problem: why after having seen so many other people healed through the laying on of my hands, after Jean's lifelong devotion to the Lord and sacrificial self-giving by my side—or rather, not by my side, but staying alone at home, whilst I engaged in itinerant ministry most of the time—why, after all this, coupled with so many prayers and partial healing, is she not fully healed?

For weeks every night after returning from the hospital in Hull I walked by the sea on the Esplanade in Scarborough asking 'Why? Why?' but I received no answer. I also prayed that the Lord would keep me from getting sour, bitter and resentful. This prayer he did answer.

The problem arises of course because some are healed and others are not and we don't know why. We will look behind the scenes so to speak to explore some possible insights into the reasons for the problems but when we have said all we know, after a lifetime of being involved, we still have problems.

First let us see why it is a problem at all. God's word gives so many bases for us to expect all to be healed— according to our faith of course. The Saviour is Jehovah-Rophi ('I am the Lord that healeth thee'). Then, now and always the same yesterday, today and for ever. The gospels often say 'he healed them all'. And Matthew insists that he healed them all in order to fulfil the prophecy of Isaiah 53:4 which refers to his atonement. The psalmist cries: 'Who forgiveth all thine iniquities; who healeth all thy diseases' (Ps 103:3); and James finalizes the matter when he says: 'the prayer of faith *shall heal the sick'*.

So, in view of all this, why are they not all healed? The answer lies, I believe, in the unbelieving traditions that have accumulated during recent centuries when there was neither faith for, nor expectation of, nor indeed any ministry of healing at all. But this is not just a contemporary problem, Jesus also accused the religious leaders of his day of, 'making the word of God of none effect through your tradition . . . and many such like things do ye' (Mk 7:13).

There are, however, a number of other reasons which people seek refuge in today.

The fellowship of his sufferings

That I may know him, and the power of his resurrection, and the fellowship of his sufferings . . . (Phil 3:10).

I remember staying in the home of two elderly sisters who were very pious Christians, and who had been in ill health for many years. After a few days I tentatively suggested that I might pray with them for healing. But oh no! They were 'sharing in the fellowship of his sufferings'.

This is a very sad misconception. In the first place suffering is not the same as sickness and disease. As far as we know, the only sickness Jesus experienced was when he bore our sicknesses in his own body on the cross. This was vicarious and there is no more sense in our trying to enter into fellowship with this than thinking of having fellowship with him in the bearing of our sins.

To teach us a lesson

There is a subtle and important difference between two

concepts in this matter. Let us acknowledge, with Job, that we can learn many lessons through sickness. But that is entirely different from the stand many take that the Lord has afflicted them to teach them a lesson.

Jesus spoke of human parents giving good gifts to their children and then adds: 'how much more shall your heavenly Father . . .' The idea of our Father putting sickness and disease on his children to teach them a lesson is preposterous, what earthly parents would put the measles (let alone cancer) on their child because it had been naughty? Yet this is not an uncommon view expressed by sick Christians.

Another thing. I always ask such people a simple question: 'What is the Lord trying to teach you?' I have never yet met anyone who has the faintest idea of what the Lord is trying to teach them! It is the strangest concept of a heavenly Father, who puts a disease on his child to teach him a lesson and then does not even tell him what he is supposed to be learning.

Nevertheless, it remains to be said, that many of God's choicest saints have found themselves shut into a life of sickness, and have testified to many blessed lessons they have learnt in such a shut in experience, not least of having proved that 'tribulation worketh patience; and patience, experience; and experience, hope: and hope maketh not ashamed; because the love of God is shed abroad in our hearts by the Holy Spirit which is given unto us' (Rom 5:3–5).

Such people of course, would make no claim to be 'choicest saints' but undoubtedly they were (are), and this process through tribulation, patience and hope has been the means—in the hands of the Holy Spirit—of producing this spiritual beauty.

Job adds his testimony to this situation, in the midst of his intense suffering before his healing, when he cries: 'Though he slay me, yet will I trust him.' Many today do just that, and it is to be highly commended, and much love and understanding should be given to all such, who are not receiving their healing largely because of reasons that are not their personal fault or responsibility, but rather because the whole body of Christ is sick and itself in need of healing.

It may not be God's will

Some people say: 'Perhaps it is not God's will to heal me—or at least now is not God's time.' I am perfectly aware that to refute this argument causes many problems for those who are not healed. I have listened to and pondered very carefully the many theological discussions about the sovereignty of God which favour this argument, but I still remain utterly convinced from Scripture that it is always God's will to heal—admitting of course that there are many other reasons why some are not healed.

Here again, many devout people hold this view, and yet invariably when they are ill and insist that it is not God's will to heal them, they nevertheless at once call in the doctor for his healing ministrations! This reminds me of a remark made by a doctor to a friend of mine. The doctor said: 'You Christians speak of the wonder and expectation of heaven in glowing terms, but the moment you look like going there, you call on me!'

If on occasion it is not God's will to heal, surely there would have been one such occasion in the three and a half years of our Lord's ministry. But never even the slightest hint of it is to be found in the gospels.

If sickness is the result of the fall, is part of the curse, is an affliction of the devil (see Acts 10:38) then why on earth should it be God's will not to heal—especially as we are fond of saying that our heavenly Father loves to give good gifts to his children and he is more willing to give than we are to receive?

The sovereignty of God

The sovereignty of God is involved in most of the things we have already discussed. His sovereignty is of course inviolable, but if we are to accept the veracity of his word as his revealed will about sickness and disease, then we cannot accept the illogicality of pitting one set of revelation against his own character and sovereignty.

There is a real problem here for our finite minds and I think it best to acknowledge that God moves in a higher dimension of thought and action than we are capable of understanding and leave it at that. With Job, let us say when we cannot understand: 'the Lord gave, and the Lord hath taken away; blessed be the name of the Lord'.

We have looked at what amount to major problems. There are mysteries in the ministry of healing that no one knows the answers to; and the more one is used in this ministry the more one acknowledges the problems and the fact that we do not know the answers.

The problems, especially the unbelieving traditions of the centuries, have created what I call a thick blanket of fog in the minds and hearts of God's people about this whole subject—a thick pea-soup fog of unbelief. Even when people confess to have real faith as they come to be prayed for, more often than not either their words or their actions (see the chapter on faith) betray that deep down there is still this blanket or fog of unbelief.

This leads us to consider the last and perhaps the most serious of the problems connected with this ministry.

The problem of preaching

Admitting that our commission is to preach the gospel and heal the sick and not to preach healing, it is nonetheless surely right in the present situation of the above mentioned problems for the servant of God who feels called to pray for the sick, first to preach on the subject. The purpose of such preaching is primarily to create a living faith in the hearts of those who wish prayer. Just here lies a deep problem.

The preacher, if his message is to be any use at all, must preach a positive faith preparing his sick hearers to come for ministry in the full expectation of receiving the Lord's healing. He must preach it positively and strongly from God's word—and that is not difficult if you are familiar with your subject.

The problem is that he must preach positively, but with the certain knowledge also in his mind, that however well taught his people may be and however well he preaches, not all who are prayed for will be healed—at least not obviously and at once. This presents a real and painful dilemma: is one to preach positive faith regardless or leave the whole subject severely alone? Alas, too many have taken the latter course. But this course of action is itself illogical. The promises of healing in God's word are no different from all the other promises in the Bible. Take sin, for instance. There are clear promises of deliverance from sin: 'sin shall not have dominion over you', for instance (Rom 6:14). It is surely right that we preach for a life of holiness and righteousness—but here again, we know that no one in our day is likely to live up to the standard of the regular Prayer Book request that 'this day we fall into no sin' or that 'henceforth we live a sober, righteous and godly life'. But despite this, no one suggests that we should no longer preach deliverance from sin. So why retreat from preaching deliverance from sickness?

In all these problems the simple answer is to acknowledge the problem but keep one's eyes upon Jesus, the author and finisher of our faith. Consider him, says the writer to the Hebrews, consider him—not the problems.

Perhaps here we may make a request to the Lord's people to pray earnestly for their preachers. They certainly need it! They have problems too!

A modern fog bank

We have looked at the problems and come to the conclusion that the sum total of them has left a thick blanket of fog of unbelief hanging over the Lord's people in the matter of healing. I find that if one has an hour's time to preach then fifty minutes are well taken up trying to blow away this blanket of fog. Leaving some ten minutes to minister a positive faith.

It is very important to grasp the fact of the fog situation. It resembles the time when it is recorded of Jesus that he could do there in his own village no mighty works because of their unbelief.

By contrast I believe we have yet to see in our country a manifestation of the 'unity of faith', when a whole congregation is really one in spirit and in positive faith for and with the sick person and those who are praying for him/her. The potential of this is enormous, and contrasts violently with the present fog situation where the majority are not only without real faith, but are more spectators than co-operators. If mass psychological situations can produce such dramatic results for evil as we see in crowd hooliganism, how much more could mass faith be used for good under the anointing of the Holy Spirit?

We come now to two instances that invariably crop up whenever the subject of healing is discussed: Job's boils and Paul's thorn in the flesh. These two, in the company of poor old Trophimas whom Paul left sick at Miletum seem to provide most folk with a satisfactory alibi for not expecting to be healed.

Job's boils

This matter is usually introduced with a question: 'What about Job and his boils?' To which I always answer: 'What about Job? He was healed!' But there are important things to learn from Job and his boils. Let us see.

It was Satan who afflicted Job. God allowed it. Satan is the author of all sickness and disease if one goes back far enough, i.e. to the effects of Adam's fall. The Pharisees asked Jesus once 'Master, who did sin, this man or his parents, that he was born blind?' (Jn 9:2). Jesus answered: 'Neither hath this man sinned, nor his parents: but that the works of God shall be made manifest in him.'

It is *possible* for sin to be the cause of sickness, as in the case when Jesus said to the man healed at the pool of Bethesda: 'sin no more, lest a worse thing come unto thee' (Jn 5:14). But it is not the normal cause of sickness.

What about Job? The main thing is that he was healed. We are given no idea as to how long he was afflicted with his boils but we are told that God allowed Satan to afflict him. God allowed it to happen to a very special person for a special reason. The reason was largely to do with Satan and not Job. Certainly Job learnt deep spiritual lessons from his illness. Maybe he had been proud before, proud of his religious rectitude. At the end when he had a new vision of the Lord God he abhorred himself and repented deeply. At least, whatever it was, in as much as he repented he must have had something to repent of!

Job was a very special person. God's report of him to Satan portrays a man of outstanding uprightness and piety. If, therefore, we want to use Job as an alibi for our sickness—or at least as a reason for our not being healed—then we need to ask ourselves how we compare with Job in character and standing before God. Can God say about you what he said to Satan about Job? (If you think he can, then God bless you!) Rather why not allow God to use your sickness to bring you to repentance and a new vision of God in Christ and then pray for your friends who have persecuted you and get your healing as Job did?

Paul's thorn in the flesh (2 Cor 12:7–9)

> And lest I should be exalted above measure through the abundance of the revelations, there was given to me a thorn in the flesh, the messenger of Satan to buffet me, lest I should be exalted above measure (2 Cor 12:7).

In order to rightly understand Paul's thorn in the flesh it is essential to keep it in context. It is part of a passage which begins in the previous chapter at verse twenty-three, where the apostle is listing his lifetime perils and tribulations while defending his own apostleship. These he then contrasts with his visions and revelations; both perils and revelations are beyond measure. In this context he says he was given a thorn in the flesh.

Here again, just in passing, notice that if we wish to hide behind Paul's thorn as an excuse for our sickness then we need—as with Job—to ask ourselves if we fit into the context: how do we match up to Paul?

The 'thorn in the flesh' was not a new phrase but

taken from Paul's intimate and extensive knowledge of the Old Testament. 'But if ye will not drive out the inhabitants of the land from before you; then it shall come to pass, that those which ye let remain of them shall be pricks in your eyes, and thorns in your sides, and shall vex you in the land wherein ye dwell' (Num 33:55). The same phrase is used again in the same connection in Joshua 23:13 and in Judges 2:3. Notice in each case that it is an external enemy troubling the people of God. This point about the thorn being something external is important and is emphasized in the context of 2 Corinthians 11:28 where Paul writes: 'Beside those things that are without, that which cometh upon me daily, the care of all the churches.'

Now let us look closely at the words used in this passage:

Infirmities (12:9). This is the Greek word *astheneia* and is the identical word translated 'weakness' in the same verse. Then in the next verse Paul lists his infirmities, namely reproaches, necessities, persecutions, and distresses—anything except *sickness*.

Weakness. Anyone, even of the strongest constitution, who has gone through the list of Paul's infirmities (i.e. 2 Cor 11:23–33) and that over many years, could hardly be anything else but weak in body as a result. What do we know of such things? Nothing at all! This was his infirmity, I have no doubt.

The messenger of Satan. This is the Greek word *angelos* and is translated in the AV 181 times by the word 'angel' and seven times as 'messenger'. In Matthew 11:10 it refers to John the Baptist as being the messenger, sent to prepare the way for the coming of Christ. In James 2:25 the 'messengers' were the two spies whom Rahab received into her house. In Revelation 12:9 it speaks of Satan and his 'angels' being cast out of heaven. From these three examples of the use of the word we conclude that it always refers to a person and not a thing.

Buffet (12:7). Dr Young in his *Concordance* indicates that this Greek word *kolaphizo* means 'to buffet with the fist'. It is a boxing word.

Bringing all this evidence together it seems obvious to me that Satan had deputed a senior and experienced 'angel' (i.e. a demon) to make it his life's work to see to it that Paul constantly had a rough time of it (cf. *The Screwtape Letters* by C. S. Lewis).

It is like when a football team has a crack player and the opposition put their best defender against him and tell him to make it his job throughout the whole match to 'look after' the crack player.

Paul's thorn therefore, as in the case of Job, was allowed by God for his own ultimate purposes, and Paul's ultimate good. I can see no valid reason for thinking Paul's thorn was a sickness or a disease. Physical weakness—yes, after such battering and no wonder!

Finally, I conclude that neither Job nor Paul, neither boils nor thorns, is a valid excuse for keeping one's sickness and disease.

9
Prophecy

Despise not prophesyings.
Prove all things; hold fast that which is good (1 Thess
5:20–21).

John Wesley, I am told, used to say that this passage—1
Thessalonians 5:16–23, was one of the most important
in the New Testament. Nevertheless, until the present
renewal (i.e. since 1960) prophecy has been despised
and the Spirit has been quenched, inasmuch as prophecy has been completely ignored and therefore unknown in the historic churches.

To obviate embarrassment on this score it has been
widely taught that prophecy is virtually synonymous
with preaching. Or alternatively, that this gift like all
the others in the NT was only to get the church off to a
good start, and then it lapsed after the first century or
so. Neither is correct. So let us define prophecy.

Two scriptures, one from the OT and one from the
NT, help us in our definitions: 'I will . . . put my words
in his mouth; and he shall speak unto them all that I
shall command him' (Deut 18:18); '. . . holy men of

God spake as they were moved by the Holy Ghost' (2 Pet 1:21). So, in the simplest of terms, prophecy is God speaking through human lips. It is like an introduction, if you will, to the very incarnation itself, which was God speaking through the full human experience of living.

From the beginning God has spoken to men. Adam said: 'I heard thy voice in the garden . . .' Before Abram moved out from Ur of the Chaldees, it is written, 'the Lord had said unto Abram . . .', and repeatedly as we follow his life story we read: 'And the Lord said to Abram . . .' I wonder how and in what way the Lord spoke to him.

To Jacob God appeared in a vision as he slept. He saw his famous 'Jacob's ladder' and we read: 'And, behold, the Lord stood above it, and said . . .'

To Moses God appeared in the burning bush and called to him out of the midst of the bush and told him of the deliverance out of Egypt he was going to effect. But after this, we read repeatedly, 'And the Lord said unto Moses . . .'

Then recounting the giving of the ten commandments Moses tells how the Lord spoke to all the assembly of the children of Israel 'out of the midst of the fire, of the cloud, and of the thick darkness, with a great voice' (Deut 5:22). At this the people were terrified, especially as they held the superstition that if any man heard the voice of God he would die as a result. Therefore they asked Moses to go near and hear all that God had to say and then report it back to them. The Lord God acquiesced in this arrangement where we may say lie the roots of this prophetic ministry.

Later in the quotation earlier in this chapter, Deuteronomy 18:18, God confirmed not only the nature and meaning of true prophecy but also the promise of its continuity. To Jeremiah God said: 'I ordained thee a prophet . . . . I shall send thee, and whatsoever I command thee thou shalt speak . . . . Then the Lord put forth his hand, and touched (his) mouth. And the Lord said . . . Behold, I have put my words in thy mouth' (Jer 1:5–9; cf. Is 6:5–10).

In all this I find it quite intriguing to imagine just how the Lord spoke to these men. Dreams and visions have undoubtedly been a major way in which God has spoken to his prophets down through the centuries. I have no experience of this and therefore refrain from further comment, except perhaps to say that in modern charismatic circles there seems to be an upsurge of rather petty visions given to all kinds of people during prayer and praise times and interpreted by others in the gathering. These may be helpful, but fall a long way short of biblical standards, as for example when Agabus took Paul's girdle and bound his own hands and feet and said, 'Thus saith the Holy Ghost, So shall the Jews at Jerusalem bind the man that owneth this girdle . . .' (Acts 21:11).

In prophecy in general it would seem that in some cases, as with Jonah, the prophet knows beforehand what he is to prophesy; but in many others he feels the urge, the inspiration to begin and the actual message is given by the Holy Spirit as he proceeds. It is here that Peter's definition is so helpful. The picture this definition gives is of a sailing ship which is propelled by the wind—'as they were moved by the Holy Ghost'—it is the prophet's job to set the sails and the Spirit will do the rest.

Prophecy, therefore, is God speaking through human lips. It is of God's initiative and man's responsibility—as Jean Darnell says: 'Responsibility is my response to his ability.' It is part of the 'partnership of the Spirit' which we have already considered in another capacity. Because of this twin nature of prophecy, it is of necessity 'according to the proportion of faith' (Rom 12:6).

Occasionally men get carried along with their own enthusiasm and pride, thinking that prophesying some spectacular thing will enhance their spiritual standing and falsely prophesy something they think to be dramatic—such as revival next year. This is like a young boy who gets a policeman's uniform outfit for a present and immediately puts it on and goes to the city centre and begins to direct the traffic! He has the outward uniform but no authority; he knows the actions but has no stature. A proper policeman comes along and says: 'Sonny, you had better go home now.'

Unfortunately, when a mature Christian speaks like this to the proud so-called prophet, the latter is usually quite indignant and accuses the other of quenching the Spirit and is often quite rude and offensive—probably proving that his prophecy was not of the Lord in any case.

In prophecy, although the word is God's, the purveyor has an important part to play and to some extent always makes his or her imprint on the finished product. God intends it to be like this. Consider the difference between the prophecy of Elijah, full of fire, and Jeremiah, full of tears.

In this connection the prophet is like a hose-pipe through which water flows. The water bears the shape of the pipe's nozzle: it may be a long spout of water, or a spray for the rose bushes. It may be a garden hose or a fire brigade hose. In each case it is a means of projecting water. So with true prophecy. It is God's word that is projected but through various kinds of channels, and according to their faith.

This leads us to consider that often prophecy is a

mixture of the true word of God and words of men. This is altogether different from the personality content mentioned in the last paragraph. The personality content does not constitute a 'mixture' element. Prophecy is, therefore, either pure, a mixture or false.

Mixed prophecy

In this matter of a mixture, as in many other things, God has decided to take a risk with men as Jesus did when he left the whole of his eternal purposes in the hands of a few men and women who were behind closed doors for fear of the Jews. It is a measure of God's confidence in the power and ministry of the Holy Spirit.

The 'mixture' may be the result of the prophet's particular brand of theology, or his church tradition, or it may reflect his emotional make-up, his ambition or his pride. This may sound alarming and it can be, but in practice most mixtures are harmless enough, consisting mainly of a few human thoughts added in amongst God's word. Often the prophecy begins in a pure way, but after the true inspiration of the Spirit has ceased, the prophet thinks it 'wise' to add a few thoughts by way of explanation or enlargement.

It is because of all this that the Bible teaches us to 'judge' prophecy, i.e. 'weigh in the balance' and to prove it and then hold fast to that which is good.

False prophecy

Immediately after the definition of prophecy quoted at the beginning of this chapter, 'I will put my words in his mouth', God goes on to warn that false prophecy would always be a possibility. God was not afraid of his risk!

The supreme test of prophecy is whether it comes to pass according to what is prophesied. If not, God says 'the prophet has spoken it presumptuously: thou shalt not be afraid of him' (Deut 18:22).

There are two grades of falsity mentioned here. In the first, the prophet presumes to speak in God's name when God has not commanded him to do so; in the second, the prophet speaks in the name of other gods. In this latter case, in OT times God said that such a prophet should be put to death, which is a measure of the gravity of saying 'thus saith the Lord' and the importance that we should attach to the true word of God.

Arthur Wallis tells of an occasion when he met a friend one Monday morning who was exuberant because of a wonderful service he had attended the day before. 'We had three prophecies,' said the man. 'It was fantastic!' 'Oh,' asked Arthur 'and what was the Lord saying in the prophecies?' The man's jaw dropped, his excitement disappeared. He had not the slightest idea of what God had been saying!

The Bible has a lot to say on the subject of false prophecy, so much in fact that I was very surprised to find how much there was. Let us consider the various different kinds and sources.

False prophecy is still with us but the vast majority of it is relatively harmless, except that it degrades the whole ministry and gives ammunition to those who oppose spiritual gifts altogether. It is mostly of the 'mixture' variety, which, as we have seen, can rely so much on human 'wisdom' that true revelation is stifled.

It is good to see what Scripture teaches, so that we may be on the alert for the future developments which are actually predicted by John to occur in the last days: 'Beloved, believe not every spirit, but try the spirits whether they are of God: because many false prophets are gone out into the world' (1 Jn 4:1; see also 2 Pet 2:1 and 2 Tim 3:1–5).

False prophecy emanates from differing sources which are clearly defined in the Scriptures.

(1) Some prophesy 'out of their own heart' (Ezek 13:17). We have touched on this earlier.

(2) Some prophesy by Baal (Jer 2:8). Originally the Baalim were supernatural beings, connected with the land and responsible for its fertility. Gradually these were amalgamated into one single divinity, Baal. Baal was later supposed to be the sun god and Ashtoreth the moon goddess. The worship of Baal included sexual orgies and homosexuality and even child sacrifices (Jer 19:4–5).

Baal worship became established by Jezebel, heathen wife of Ahab; it was put down by Elijah, but persisted sporadically long after that (Jer 19:5). Like all heathen worship, Baal had its priests and prophets who prophesied, no doubt under the influence of evil spirits (Jer 23:13).

(3) Some prophesy by a lying spirit (1 Kings 22:22–23). The unexpected feature of this incident is that the Lord acquiesced in this for his own good reasons.

(4) Some, out of the deceit of their hearts, prophesy by divination, 'a false vision and divination, and a thing of nought, and the deceit of their heart' (Jer 14:14). Divination is simply fortune-telling and soothsaying. Sometimes the diviner went into a form of trance, real or pretended, and claimed to have mystic awareness of coming events (see Acts 16:16). Divination was specifically forbidden under the law of Moses, along with 'observers of times, enchanters and witches' (see Deut 18:10–12). All these, like the prophets of Baal, were under the influence of evil spirits. This was also the practice of Simon the sorcerer, in Samaria, as recorded

in Acts 8:9–24.

There are many such prophets today associated with spiritism (also called spiritualism). Evil spirits do have both supernatural power and knowledge and deceive many who insist they are good spirits, by their healing ability and reputedly bringing back the spirits of (recent) deceased loved ones. These practices are an abomination to the Lord. As always Satan gets as near as possible to the true activities of the Holy Spirit. He is a liar from the beginning.

(5) Some prophesy as a cover for secret sin, often of a dreadful kind; they are wolves in sheep's clothing. 'I have seen folly in the prophets of Samaria . . . I have seen also in the prophets of Jerusalem an horrible thing: they commit adultery, and walk in lies: they strengthen also the hands of evildoers' (Jer 23:13–14).

(6) Finally, following his usual tactics of trying to be as near to the genuine divine thing as possible, Satan even produces prophecies accompanied by signs and wonders. God warned the children of Israel against this in Deuteronomy 13:1–3, and Jesus included the warning in his discourse about the events leading up to the second coming. 'And many false prophets shall rise, and shall deceive many,' he said. 'For there shall arise false Christs, and false prophets, and shall shew great signs and wonders; insomuch that, if it were possible, they shall deceive the very elect' (Mt 24:11, 24). It appears from this that such prophesying might well occur amongst the very elect. So we need to beware. 'Behold, I have told you before' adds the master.

Paul, writing to the Thessalonians, also warns the brethren against the danger of falling away, which presumably means that some will be amongst the Lord's people when such things happen namely: 'the working of Satan with all power and signs and lying wonders, and with all deceivableness of unrighteousness' (2 Thess 2:9–10). 'Know also,' says Paul to Timothy, 'that in the last days perilous times shall come' (2 Tim 3:1) and John echoes: 'it is the last time . . . even now there are many antichrists . . . they went out from us' (1 Jn 2:18).

It may be thought that such things could never happen in our current situations but Jesus thought it necessary to warn us of the danger: 'Beware of false prophets . . . ravening wolves . . . a corrupt tree bringeth forth evil fruit' (Mt 7:15–20). Yet as we walk in the Spirit and retain the anointing from the Holy One we need have no fear of these abominable counterfeits and it is not good to dwell on such negative possibilities; however, inasmuch as Scripture has so much to say on the subject, it is good that at least we be alerted because Satan is a very clever devil!

To return to more mundane matters amongst us as the Lord's renewed people, we nonetheless need to apply the scriptural safeguards in relation to this important ministry. 'Despise not prophesyings. Prove all things; hold fast that which is good' (1 Thess 5:20–21). 'Let the prophets speak,' says Paul '. . . and let the other judge' (1 Cor 14:29). As to how we are to judge, various standards are given. Basically we are to check if what is prophesied comes to pass or not (Deut 18), how it stands in relation to our loving the Lord (Deut 13) and then the moral standing of the one who prophesies is to be checked.

Everything to do with spiritual gifts needs to come very much under the lordship of Christ, as Paul emphasizes in his opening passage on the subject (1 Cor 12:3). In addition, every prophecy must be tested according to its accord with the written word (1 Cor 14:37). The prophets must accept the judgement of those whom

God has set in authority in the local church—and if they refuse to accept any correction it is obvious that something is sadly wrong. This is covered by the overall instruction for everything to be done decently and in order (1 Cor 14:40).

There are many examples of prophecy in the NT beginning with Zacharias who 'was filled with the Holy Ghost, and prophesied' (Lk 1:67). Prophecy was central in Joel's prophecy (Joel 2:28–29) quoted by Peter on the day of Pentecost and it is interesting to note that in the last days both sons and daughters are to prophesy. This prophecy was reinforced by the apostle when he spoke in 1 Corinthians 11:5 about every woman that 'prayeth or prophesieth'. (How many are dishonouring their heads in the process is not our concern at the moment!)

Philip, the evangelist, had four daughters who prophesied, and Agabus was an acknowledged prophet in the early church. He fulfilled the test as to whether his prophecy came to pass. In the church at Antioch there were both teachers and prophets. Judas and Silas are mentioned as prophets who 'exhorted the brethren with many words, and confirmed them' (Acts 15:32).

Ignatius of Antioch writing to Philadelphia refers to 'the time I was with you, I cried out with a loud voice—the very voice of God'. It is also reported of Melito of Sardis that in the middle of his preaching he went into the first person, i.e. he moved over from preaching to prophesying.

This raises the whole question of how to word prophecy, whether in direct or indirect speech. It probably depends on the dimension of the prophecy (see later). In Antioch, assuming as I do, that when it says 'the Holy Ghost said' it means prophecy, the prophet spoke directly and authoritatively in the first person, i.e. God himself was the speaker: 'Separate me Barnabas and Saul for the work whereunto I have called them' (Acts 13:2).

When Agabus prophesied it is recorded that he said: 'Thus saith the Holy Ghost . . .' This is the NT equivalent of 'Thus saith the Lord' (Ezek 29:3). Paul, on the other hand, though an apostle and not a prophet, uses the phrase: 'this we say unto you by the word of the Lord . . .' (1 Thess 4:15).

The use of the first person, usually 'Thus saith the Lord', is fairly common in some circles today, but sometimes one wonders if those who use it have ever stopped to think of the enormity of such an assertion. Prophecy according to Romans 12:6 is to be 'according to the proportion of faith' and also with all gifts, 'according to the grace that is given to us'. If taken seriously, it takes a bold man to claim sufficient grace and faith to use such words in public. Yet it can and should be done, under the Spirit's direction, and one could say we are sadly in need of such a voice from above.

Agabus on another occasion is reported by Luke to have 'signified by the Spirit' and certain disciples at Tyre 'said to Paul through the Spirit . . .' We may say that these two examples are in the first person but not quite so strongly as 'Thus saith the Lord'.

On the whole, as far as the gift of prophecy is concerned it would certainly be better to use indirect speech, such as 'The Lord is saying . . .' or 'The Holy Spirit is saying . . .' Inasmuch as all prophecy is to be judged, it is equally good, as some do, to say 'I feel the Holy Spirit is saying . . .'

The dimensions of prophecy

It is wise and scriptural to differentiate between differ-

ent levels of prophecy. They can be classified as follows:
1) A prophet;
2) The gift of prophecy;
3) The spirit of prophecy—where all may prophesy.

A prophet

This is one of the five gifts of the ascended Christ, given to the body of Christ (Eph 4:8–11). It is through a prophet that we may expect to hear the authoritative voice of the head of the church speaking to his people. Along with the other four ministries this is given 'for the perfecting of the saints, for the work of the ministry'. They are given to lead the Lord's people into spiritual unity, and to safeguard them from 'every wind of doctrine'.

When introducing these ascension gifts the apostle quotes from Psalm 68:18 'When he ascended up on high, he led captivity captive . . .' In the same breath the psalmist adds (but this is not quoted by Paul) 'yea, for the rebellious also, that the Lord God might dwell among them'.

From the beginning God's main desire seems to have been to dwell amongst his people. God walked in the garden with Adam; he also spoke to Moses with very strict instructions to build a tabernacle with an ark and a mercy seat saying: 'let them make me a sanctuary; that I may dwell among them' (Ex 25:8) and all this in spite of all the rebellion from that day to this.

The five-fold ministers of Ephesians 4 are Christ's representatives in his body, to be the main implementers of his headship—and the prophet is one of the five. But side by side with this revelation the apostle reminds us of 'that which every joint supplieth, according to the effectual working in the measure of every part'.

In the OT the prophet often had a message to the nation, or even the nations; in the NT there is no indication that this is still the case, although Agabus did prophesy that there would be a great dearth throughout all the world which came to pass in the days of Claudius Caesar.

In the NT it does seem that the prophet sometimes speaks personally to individuals in a decisive manner, as for instance in Acts 13, where Barnabas and Saul are called to be separated to the work to which the Lord had called them. Inasmuch as the past tense is used, it suggests that this was a call confirming what had previously been personally revealed to the two men by the Holy Spirit. Again, in Acts 21, the prophet Agabus is used to speak personally to the apostle Paul about future events in his life.

Another aspect of the ministry of a true prophet is emphasized by Paul in the Ephesian epistle. Twice in this epistle the prophets' ministry is linked in an intimate way with that of the apostles. First in a foundational manner, and secondly in the sphere of revelation. We regularly take the word 'now' of the epistles to apply to our modern 'now', for example in Ephesians 3:10, and I see no reason why the same should not be true with regard to the matter of revelation in Ephesians 3:5 either.

It would seem as though God has linked these two ministries closely together as in the case of Paul and Barnabas (Acts 13) and later Paul and Silas (Acts 15:40; see also verse 32). And at the end of 1 Corinthians 12 the apostle asks: 'Are all apostles? are all prophets?'

The prophet's ministry is essentially inspirational, and as such he needs another by his side to expound correctly and put in proper context the inspired word.

A prophet must be able to be especially sensitive to the inner voice of the Spirit; but this also makes him particularly aware of the powers of darkness that oppose God's will in the spiritual warfare in which pioneers are particularly engaged. This makes it all the more necessary for the prophet to have the more stable, down to earth, pioneering ministry of an apostle by his side.

The gift of prophecy

Elsewhere we have maintained that any gift of the Spirit is available to any Spirit-filled member of the body of Christ, and this is covered by our third dimension; but it is also true in practice that often one person receives a special ministry along the line of one particular gift. One is regularly used in healing; another in a word of wisdom. So here one person is much used on a fairly regular basis to prophesy.

It is in this connection that the apostle teaches that such prophecy is for the three-fold purpose of edification, exhortation and comfort (1 Cor 14:3). All the gifts are to concentrate on edification but this is to be especially true of the gift of prophecy. It is this which occasions the apostle's often quoted remark that he would rather speak five words with the understanding than ten thousand in a tongue (1 Cor 14:19).

Edification basically means a building up of the edifice, the church, i.e. the members of Christ's body, not the church building—the building metaphor is used in a different way than is current today. In the last resort, the only way to build a building is to add one stone on to another. So if through prophecy the secrets of a non-Christian's (unlearned) heart are revealed and consequently he admits that God is truly with his people, then presumably he will join them and so another stone will be added to the mystical body. That is edification.

Of course edification has the more general meaning of building up in the most holy faith of the Lord's people. 'Exhortation' is an interesting word too. It is *paraklesis* which is a normal word for comfort whereas the word comfort in this passage is *paramuthia* which means a consolation. *Paraklesis* is the same root word as 'comforter' used in John's gospel for the Holy Spirit, meaning one who draws alongside.

So we judge that the gift of prophecy is (1) for outreach and the building up of the body of Christ; (2) for comfort, in the sense of strengthening together (Latin, *con* + *fortis*) through the ministry of the Holy Spirit and (3) general consolation for those in trouble and distress. In some cases prophecy along these lines can be personal, for a particular person with a special need or in a particular predicament, but mostly it will be of a general nature.

I remember once hearing a prophecy which was both loving and entreating and yet very severe, addressed to one man by name inviting him not to continue to resist the Holy Spirit but to yield his life to Christ. This he did, to the saving of his marriage and every other blessing of a new life in Christ. Such occasions however are very rare and should not be embarked upon without very strong promptings of the Holy Spirit and every available precaution.

The spirit of prophecy

This is a phrase I have coined to describe Paul's words which say: 'Ye may all prophesy.' Such ministry is certainly not that of a prophet. Some may prefer to think of it as just the occasional use of the gift of prophecy but, as mentioned earlier, some seem to have been given this gift to use in a fairly regular way and therefore develop in maturity in this exercise. The use of the phrase 'the spirit of prophecy' is to provide a distinction between the occasional and the more regular mature ministry.

Those who minister in this way are usually just beginning, and do so very simply and tentatively, in fear and trembling; it is very often acceptably done under the real anointing of the Holy Spirit and because it is not a commonplace to the person is usually untarnished by any human content—in short it is very blessed.

All of this underlines a basic principle for prophecy, which is set out by the apostle in Romans 12:6, that one is to prophesy according to the proportion of faith; this in turn means that one has to begin, to step out in faith for the first time. As with everything to do with faith, it will grow and mature, this of course happens chiefly by usage.

Whatever the dimension or depth of the ministry of prophecy let all who prophesy remember that it is for holy men of God to be moved, to be blown along by the wind of the Holy Spirit, and that true prophecy is a word from the Lord through human lips. Let them seek by every possible way, especially their manner of life and spiritual development, to make their words just that, neither more nor less. Let them accept graciously that their words are to be weighed in the balance by others and that everything has to be done decently and in order, which means, among other things, under the direction and control of the leadership at the time.

Let those who hear and those who judge see to it that they give due respect to a word from the Lord, in short that they be careful not to despise prophesyings.

10

The Word of Wisdom and the Word of Knowledge

> For to one is given by the Spirit the word of wisdom; to another the word of knowledge by the same Spirit (1 Cor 12:8).

These two gifts are so interdependent that it will be wise to consider them together. It is interesting to note that the word of wisdom is mentioned first, although logically knowledge comes first. Let us see the difference between the two. There is a lot to say later in this chapter about the kind of wisdom and knowledge which constitute the *charismata*; but for the moment let us clarify the difference in general terms.

Knowledge is the sum total of what is known, the range of information; in other words: the facts. Wisdom is based on knowledge; it is possessing knowledge and experience together with the ability to apply such knowledge and experience critically and practically and wisely.

My headmaster at school was an extremely clever man. His knowledge was very extensive, but he was a hopeless teacher. When he put his knowledge into words they were way above the heads of his pupils. His word of wisdom was minimal.

Ananias received knowledge from the Lord in a vision so he was then able to speak a word of knowledge; but he manifested a word of wisdom by the way he expressed his knowledge (Acts 9:10–17). Remembering that as far as he and everybody else knew, Saul was still breathing out threatenings and slaughter, Ananias went into him, laid his hands upon him and said, 'Brother Saul . . .' that expressed both courage, love and faith. It was a word of wisdom.

To look now at these twin *charismata,* the first essential is to note that both have to do with words. The gifts are not knowledge and wisdom but the word of knowledge and the word of wisdom; that is, it is spoken knowledge and spoken wisdom.

The word of knowledge

There are numerous examples of this gift in the OT. A few examples will suffice. Samuel, it is recorded had been a 'seer' and no doubt received his knowledge in this way. But in his time seers became known as 'prophets', i.e. those who 'spoke out' what they had 'seen' (1 Sam 9:9). God had given him knowledge that Saul's asses had been found; and that Saul was to be the first king of Israel (1 Sam 9:15–16). He then expressed this knowledge to Saul in word.

Elisha had a tremendous capacity as a seer. He knew that Gehazi had followed Naaman to receive money (2 Kings 5:26); he knew what the king of Syria was saying in his council of war (2 Kings 6:8–9): because he had knowledge he spoke and told Gehazi that he would be a leper for his greed, and he told the king of Israel where the Syrians planned to engage in battle.

In the NT Jesus was also a seer and a prophet. He saw Nathanael under the fig tree, though not with his natural eyes, and spoke it out, to win an early disciple (Jn 1:48–50). Jesus exercised the gift of the word of knowledge when he spoke to the woman at the well: 'Jesus said unto her . . . thou hast had five husbands' (Jn 4:17–18).

Peter knew by the Holy Spirit that Ananias and Sapphira had agreed to lie about the price of the land they had sold—and he spoke it out with devastating consequences (Acts 5:3–5, 8–10).

However, I am convinced that in the church, the body of Christ the twin *charismata* have to do primarily with preaching and teaching. This will be our main theme in this chapter. There are however other uses of these gifts and it will be well to examine these briefly first.

As a prelude to healing

This has become very popular recently. It is part of the general lusting after the spectacular, failing to understand that for something to be supernatural it does not always have to be spectacular.

The way it goes is something like this: the one claiming to be exercising the gift of the word of knowledge will announce that there is someone in the congregation with an affliction in, say, the left eye, or the right knee—or wherever. Some claim that they can actually feel the affliction themselves in whatever part of the body is mentioned and this is the way the Spirit gives them this knowledge. The person with such an affliction is then expected to acknowledge it publicly and thereupon he is declared to be healed. Undoubtedly the word of knowledge does actually come in this or some similar way on occasion, but I can think of no example of it in the NT and to me that makes it suspect. But when all kinds of leaders start to copy this routine and also widen its scope to include more common complaints and refer to larger numbers of people—say, five or six people with a headache or pains in the back—then by the law of averages one does not need a word of knowledge to be correct. And if the leader is persuasive enough it is not difficult to get the required response. It *can* be a word of knowledge, but as with prophecy it is wise to 'let others judge'.

In leading divine worship

Years ago I was leader, an equal amongst other 'elders', and during an elders' meeting one man had strongly disagreed with the rest of us about some matter. So much so, that unknown to us he had gone home and written out his resignation. On further reflection and after a time of prayer he altered his letter to read that unless we were singing one particular hymn as he arrived late for the next Sunday morning service then he would resign. The hymn was not one at all suitable for a holy communion service. If we were singing that hymn then he would accept correction from the Holy Spirit and say nothing more about resignation. I was leading the worship and, ignorant of his letter and against all my better judgement, I felt strongly that we should begin with this particular hymn and announced it. As we sang the third verse the elder walked in and came straight to the front and asked permission to speak. He told us what had happened in humility and repentance. We prayed with him and rejoiced together. I consider that when I announced that hymn I was responding to a word of knowledge.

On another occasion, during a campaign in South Wales, as we were singing 'Love divine all loves excel-

ling' to the tune of Blaenwern (as only a Welsh congregation can sing such a hymn) I noticed a well-known
gospel singer whom I knew well, arriving late. After we
had sung many verses many times I asked the gospel
singer to sing us a verse as a solo. Quite unknown to me
she had arrived late because she had a very heavy cold
and had completely lost her voice—even to speak, let
alone sing—however faith was running high, the presence of the Lord was real and she had already in
previous meetings been much uplifted in faith, so she
stood to her feet when I asked for the solo, opened her
mouth in simple faith and sang as beautifully as she had
ever done before! And she was healed from her cold
into the bargain. My request was a word of knowledge.

In administration

This has to do with parochial church councils, deacons'
meetings and the like—whatever they are called in your
fellowship.

Among the *charismata* of Romans 12, is the ministry
of 'ruling'. 'He that ruleth', says the apostle, should do
it 'with diligence'. The word means to be 'set over' as a
father is in his own home, and in the church this ministry obviously refers to those who have the job of administration.

Such committee meetings, alas, are often conducted
no differently from a business board meeting and decisions are taken purely on a commonsense basis, often
dictated more by the lack of finance than any seeking
and finding the mind of the Lord. Unfortunately,
frayed tempers often manifest themselves in unkind
words and selfish attitudes as well—in short 'such
wisdom descendeth not from above'. There is a per-
functory prayer at the start and the 'grace' at the end
and that is that.

How different it can be, and happily I speak from experience. We used to meet, seven to ten of us, every week. After briefly detailing any matters that needed our attention, we would then turn to prayer and praise for an hour or so. We worshipped and sought the guidance of the Holy Spirit and—though not in so many words—we requested the gifts of the word of knowledge and the word of wisdom.

Almost invariably as we turned to consider the relevant matters we found that we were all of the same mind. We had the mind of Christ according to his promise. We continued then in fellowship and inevitable cups of tea, with never a wrong word. The first hour of course was the key to all our success.

When before hostile authorities

> And ye shall be brought before governors and kings for my sake. . . But when they deliver you up, take no thought how or what ye shall speak: for it shall be given you in that same hour what ye shall speak. For it is not ye that speak, but the Spirit of your Father which speaketh in you (Mt 10:18–20).

Fortunately for us in the West this has little significance at present. Some think this state will not last for much longer. Time alone will tell. But there are many parts of the world where the faithful members of the body of Christ are very often hauled before the powers that be on account of their allegiance to Christ and these promises quoted above are a very precious manifestation of the twin gifts we are considering. Corrie Ten Boom's experience during the war is a wonderful testimony to this provision of our heavenly Father for his children in times of trouble and danger.

In an increasingly pagan UK this may well become more and more important, not so much before hostile governments, but unsympathetic employers and managers at all levels.

In counselling situations

The nearest example in the NT to what we now call counselling is surely the story of our Lord talking with the woman at the well in John 4. Here, very clearly, both the gift of the word of knowledge and the word of wisdom are in evidence. We may extend this section to include *witnessing* as well as counselling. There is a great need (as we shall see later) to lift so many of our normal Christian routines into a much more spiritual dimension. So much is still attempted at every level by relying to a large extent on human ability and experience.

My friend, the late Edgar Trout once had the remarkable experience of knowing by the gift of knowledge that a woman who had asked to see him was actually a consummate liar and also a prostitute—and the Holy Spirit insisted that he should tell her that he knew!

That was exceptional; but quite often when counselling I have been led to ask some question or make some remark that on the face of it was quite ordinary but which has produced an immediate reaction: 'How did you know to ask (or say) that?' Only by the Holy Spirit. But that was the key to unlock the problem and lead to deliverance.

So in many ways we need very much to take heed to the scripture which tells us not to 'lean . . . unto thine own understanding', but rather in all our ways to acknowledge him and thereby find that he is directing our paths (Prov 3:5–6).

In preaching and teaching

Now I return to the main thrust of this chapter, namely

that I am convinced that the twin gifts of the word of knowledge and wisdom are primarily the Lord's provision for effective preaching and teaching.

We have been so conditioned to expect all the gifts of the Spirit to be wholly supernatural (which in turn we have wrongly interpreted to mean they should be spectacular), that we have forgotten that the greatest miracles of all, namely regenerated and changed lives, are the result of preaching: 'it pleased God by the foolishness of preaching to save them that believe' (1 Cor 1:21).

Not only is dynamic, Holy Spirit inspired preaching a very rare art these days, but there also seems to be a wholesale tendency to copy the world and *emphasize dialogue*—which is considered to be superior—at the expense of preaching. My experience of dialogue, and the inevitable seminars about it, is that every Tom, Dick and Harry expresses his or her view and we rarely come to any consensus, and even if we do I have found no transforming power in it all.

The gifts of the Spirit are to be regarded as the Holy Spirit in action. That is correct. But the scriptural description of this is, 'they went forth, and preached every where, the Lord working with them, and confirming the word with signs following' (Mk 16:20). That is a very accurate description of the whole ministry of the apostles in Luke's account in the Acts of the Apostles. In a word: the action—the supernatural—was the confirmation of the word.

The word was all-important. Are we to expect the confirmation to be of the Spirit and powerful and the word be less so? Surely not! Yet, we have allowed the preaching of the word to descend to being little more than an intellectual exercise, and training for the ministry to be almost wholly along the same lines.

There is nothing wrong with training the mind of course; indeed it is to be commended—so long as it is understood that it is training to better the preacher's part in the partnership, which, we have found, was the Holy Spirit taking control of and using any and every human faculty.

Peter had no intellectual training, yet his message on the day of Pentecost was packed full of words of knowledge far beyond his own capacity; and the result was what Jesus promised it would be, that when the Holy Spirit came he would convict of sin, righteousness and judgement (Jn 16:8–11).

Paul, on the other hand, had had the very best of intellectual training. What then does he do with it?

> And I, brethren, when I came to you, came not with excellency of speech or of wisdom, declaring unto you the testimony of God. For I determined not to know anything among you, save Jesus Christ, and him crucified. And I was with you in weakness, and in fear, and in much trembling. And my speech and my preaching was not with enticing words of man's wisdom, but in demonstration of the Spirit and of power: that your faith should not stand in the wisdom of men, but in the power of God (1 Cor 2:1–5).

Indeed the whole of the first two chapters of 1 Corinthians are an exposition of the nature, meaning and use of the gifts of the word of wisdom and knowledge.

The content of the word of knowledge

'The preaching of the cross is to them that perish foolishness; but unto us which are saved it is the power of God'—it is a foolishness of God that is wiser than men. The preaching of the cross is the power of God and the wisdom of God.

Philip went down to Samaria and preached Christ to

them. They gave heed to those things which he spoke, because they heard and saw the miracles, the confirmation of the word. The upshot was that they believed Philip's preaching of the things concerning the kingdom of God and the name of Jesus Christ and were baptized (see Acts 8:5–12).

I remember hearing of a preacher in America who had a teenage son who was afflicted so that his head was like a lump of jelly. He was quite uncontrolled and unable to speak. His eyes rolled uncontrollably. He was totally pathetic. The preacher was baptized in the Holy Spirit and God healed his son, a fantastic miracle. He went almost immediately to his church's annual synod expecting to win his fellow preachers over to believe in charismatic things. Many of the synod had seen this unfortunate boy before. Now he was standing at his father's side, healed and perfectly normal. The preacher gave his testimony. It was received in stony silence and the chairman suggested that they get on with the agenda. Such things did not fit in with their theology. It is not miracles that transform and bring in the kingdom but the preaching of the word.

Stephen was full of faith and power and did great wonders and miracles among the people. But the Scriptures add: 'they were not able to resist the wisdom and the spirit by which he spake'. Ultimately he was called before the high priest and the council to defend himself. It is recorded that 'when they heard these things, they were cut to the heart'. To human logic I would say he had preached a rather long rambling sermon on the history of the children of Israel (see Acts 7:2–53). It had little to commend it to a trained intellect but it concluded with a revelation of the exalted Christ; it must have been given with great power and under the anointing of the Holy Spirit for it deeply convicted an unbelieving and hostile audience.

The contrast with man's wisdom

The apostle insists that he preached in Corinth 'not with enticing words of man's wisdom' or with 'excellency of speech or of wisdom'. 'We speak wisdom,' he says, 'the wisdom of God in a mystery'; it was wisdom which God had revealed to him by the Spirit. To the Galatians he said, 'when it pleased God . . . to reveal his Son in me, that I might preach him among the heathen, immediately I conferred not with flesh and blood: neither went I up to Jerusalem to them which were apostles before me . . .' (Gal 1:15–17).

Notice the recurrence of 'speech', 'preach' and 'words' in all these quotations and in the whole of 1 Corinthians 2: 'Which things also we *speak*, not in the *words* which man's wisdom teacheth . . . (because) the natural man receiveth not the things of the Spirit of God: for they are foolishness unto him: neither can he know them, because they are spiritually discerned. . . But we have the mind of Christ' (verses 13–16).

Now, we rightly think today of the 'word' as being God's word especially the NT, but we must remember that the early preachers had no NT. If our intellectual training develops our capability of understanding God's word, then that is all to the good—so long as our intellect does not thereby become the source of our understanding. It is the Holy Spirit that 'searcheth all things, yea, the deep things of God' (1 Cor 2:10).

Purely as man to man, says Paul, you cannot know what is in my mind; even so only the Spirit of God knows 'the deep things of God', which things are freely given to us that we might *speak* them in *words,* not what man's wisdom teaches but what the Holy Spirit teaches. The whole emphasis is on *words*. They are words of wisdom and words of knowledge.

Wherever Paul went he preached. Looking back over his ministry at Ephesus he said: 'I have kept back nothing . . . but . . . have taught you publickly, and from house to house, testifying . . . the gospel of the grace of God . . . preaching the kingdom of God' (Acts 20:20–25). At the end of Acts it is reported that he was still 'preaching the kingdom of God and teaching those things which concern the Lord Jesus Christ' in his own hired house while a prisoner in Rome.

We may well ask: 'Where does all this leave the preacher—and the concept and content of teaching now?'

Certainly historically-speaking the church has got it right in making preaching its main ministry. Paul's instruction to young Timothy was 'Preach the word; be instant in season, out of season. . .' (2 Tim 4:2). And as for himself, he insists time and again: 'Christ sent me not to baptize, but to preach the gospel' (1 Cor 1:17); 'to make the Gentiles obedient, by word and deed, through mighty signs and wonders, by the power of the Spirit of God; so . . . I have fully preached the gospel of Christ' (Rom 15:18–19).

The church has rightly set great store upon preserving the 'truth'. I was proud of my knowledge of and preaching of the 'truth', fully accepting what we now call 'charismatic truth' long before the days of charismatic renewal, and I rather tended to look down on those who did not preach 'the whole counsel of God', meaning (to me) accepting the whole of the NT as God's truth for the church today.

My self-satisfaction received a considerable jolt, however, one day when the Holy Spirit took me to the words of Jesus: 'ye shall know the truth, and the truth

shall make you free'. I felt the Spirit asking and re-
fusing to be put off with a side-stepping answer: 'When
did the truth you preach last set anyone free?' I had no
answer. It hadn't. From there, in my chastened state,
the Spirit took me to 2 Corinthians 3:6, 'Who also hath
made us able ministers of the new testament; not of the
letter, but of the spirit: for the letter killeth, but the
spirit giveth life.' The Spirit then showed me and convicted me that correct biblical exegesis in the purely
intellectual sense can still be 'of the letter'. This seems
to be the thrust of the rest of 2 Corinthians 3, where the
apostle refers to the Jews who regularly read the OT—
which surely is God's truth—and yet whose hearts were
veiled and to whom it ministered only condemnation
and death.

By contrast, Jesus said: 'It is the spirit that quicken-
eth; the flesh profiteth nothing: the words that I speak
unto you, they are spirit, and they are life' (Jn 6:63).
After that saying it is recorded that 'many of his disciples went back, and walked no more with him'. Jesus
then asked the twelve 'Will ye also go away?' Peter
answered: 'Lord, to whom shall we go? thou hast the
words of eternal life.'

The purpose of the twin gifts of the word of wisdom
and knowledge is that the preacher's words shall also be
'spirit and life', the words of eternal life.

Amongst all this, I feel that it calls for a much greater
dependence on the guidance and prompting of the Holy
Spirit whilst the preacher is on his feet in the pulpit.
This is in no way to suggest that adequate preparation
should be done away with, rather that we should be
open for redirection of what we have prepared—or on
occasion even a complete change of subject.

I was called to take a series of services in Hudders-
field. First there were only about twelve people in the

congregation but the word began to work and soon the church (though only small) was full. Among those who began to attend were a man and wife who had been Christadelphians. The man was self-educated and quite sure of himself and only came because of his wife. She had been born again and quite transformed, so much so that her husband just had to acknowledge the miracle.

After a while as conviction began to burn in the man's soul he went to his bedroom, opened a Bible at random and put his finger on a verse which he wrote down on a piece of paper, put it in an envelope and sealed it and then gave it to his wife. He then knelt and prayed that if what this chap was preaching was the 'truth' and Christ was real and present with him, then he asked God to cause him to preach from that verse next Sunday night.

On that Sunday night I stood to preach what I had prepared but my mind went a complete blank. I stood silent for a moment or two feeling very embarrassed. I began to turn the pages of my Bible, when suddenly one verse stood out from all the rest. I felt strongly I was to preach from that verse, which I did. After I had finished the Christadelphian came forward and told the story I have just related. I had preached on the verse in the sealed envelope! He gave his life to Christ as a result.

For this sort of preaching to be possible, we need to be fully conversant with the word of God, it needs to be 'dwelling in our hearts richly', and like Jesus in his own synagogue, we need to be able to open the book and find the place (Lk 4:17).

My Christadelphian story is exceptional of course. But if we really believe we can have these twin gifts to transform our preaching, bringing it into the dimension of spirit and life, and such as will be confirmed with signs following, then we will have to learn to be much more dependent on the Holy Spirit both in our preparation and also when actually in the pulpit. Furthermore, we will have to be soaked in the word of God so that the Holy Spirit can draw upon God's word which is permanently resident in our hearts and minds.

Being slavishly tied to a prepared manuscript will be a thing of the past, rather, we will be like the apostle Paul, who said, 'having the same spirit of faith . . . we also believe, and therefore speak . . . .' (2 Cor 4:13); that is: we believe (a) that God has made us able ministers of the new covenant and (b) we are those to whom are given the words of wisdom and knowledge. It was Paul's prayer that the Father may give us 'the spirit of wisdom and revelation in the knowledge of him: the eyes of (our) understanding being enlightened' (Eph 1:17–18). The Holy Spirit will be our guide in this regard.

11

The Discerning of Spirits

The Greek word for 'discerning' carries the idea of making a difference, to distinguish between different things.

It is to be emphasized that this gift is the discerning of spirits and not a judgement (discerning) of people.

There are three main realms of spirit activity: the human spirit, evil spirits, and the Holy Spirit. From this it follows that everything that is not right does not necessarily have to be evil, it may well be and often is, merely an activity or speaking out from the human spirit. If the person in question has the Holy Spirit indwelling them, as is usually the case, then as often as not no serious damage is done. Unfortunately, far too often one feels that what goes as prophecy is done on this basis. It consists of scriptural quotations or simple thoughts on such quotations, which can be very nice, and even inspiring to some extent but which is not real prophecy. If this happens in a public service it is best just to take what is good out of the so-called prophecy without comment and carry on with the service. If it persists regularly it can be lovingly dealt with privately.

The activity of evil spirits, of course, is quite another matter. Here the gift of discernment is most essential because, as Jesus indicated, many an evil spirit masquerades as a good spirit, even as the Holy Spirit.

It was our habit in one church where I was the leader to pray for the sick quite regularly at the front of the church; a few of the congregation who felt the Lord was leading them in this ministry, often joined me and the other leaders as we prayed for the sick with the laying on of hands. A stranger started to attend our services regularly, acting circumspectly in every way, sometimes praying aloud at the appropriate time. After a while he asked politely if he might join the group praying for the sick as he felt he had some ministry in this sphere. I agreed, only to learn some weeks later, from something he said to me in private conversation, that he was a spiritist! To my shame I had been completely deceived. We stopped any further participation in the healing ministry and soon he left and we never saw him again.

Once a friend and I were taking an afternoon prayer meeting somewhere in South Wales. It was very informal and Philip, my friend, had walked to the back of the hall and was standing there. All of a sudden a woman kneeling at the front row began to speak in a tongue. It was a horrible, blood-curdling tongue. I immediately went and laid hands on her, whereupon she stopped. After a few minutes another woman near the front started to speak in the same tongue. She, too, stopped when I laid hands on her. Philip meanwhile returned to my side at the altar and told me that when I laid hands on the first woman he actually saw a nebulous something (he hadn't a word for it) come out of the woman. It wormed its way like a snake to the back of the hall and then returned and disappeared into the second woman, whereupon she began her tongue. Needless to say we cast this evil spirit out on the spot, prayed for the two women and the first later spoke in a lovely tongue by the Holy Spirit.

I tell this story to illustrate that there are many ways in which the Holy Spirit can give us discernment of evil spirits—such as Philip's remarkable experience seeing this thing. Philip is a true 'seer', a prophet indeed, in any case, as well as having the gift of discerning of spirits.

On another occasion, I was ministering at a conference in Devon with Jean Darnall. She was preaching and I was called out into another room to pray for a lady for healing. She was in a bad way. She told us a sad story: for months now she had been sick all the time with various sores and illnesses. No sooner had she got over one illness than another took hold of her, time and time again. I sought the Lord's leading and it was revealed that, like the woman in Luke 13, she had a 'spirit of infirmity'. Jesus said to the woman, 'Woman thou art loosed from thine infirmity.' And he laid his hands on her and immediately she was made straight, and glorified God. I did exactly the same in Devon and the woman was healed and had no further trouble.

When the apostle Paul was in Philippi on his first missionary journey, a woman started to follow him and cried out saying: 'These men are the servants of the most high God, which show unto us the way of salvation.' Now this was perfectly true, there was no falsehood in this at all; yet Paul, through the gift of discerning of spirits, perceived that she was speaking out from a spirit of divination and after a few days he turned and said to the spirit: 'I command thee in the name of Jesus Christ to come out of her.' And it came out 'the same hour' (Acts 16:16–18).

That is one thing. But John warns us that many false spirits have gone out into the world and Paul says to Timothy that the Holy Spirit speaks expressly that 'in the latter times [that is now!] some shall depart from the faith, giving heed to seducing spirits, and doctrines of devils; speaking lies in hypocrisy . . .' (1 Tim 4:1–2). And to Titus the apostle adds: 'For there are many unruly and vain talkers and deceivers, specially they of the circumcision' (Tit 1:10).

All this is very important and terribly relevant today, for not only is spiritism a very real power in the land and on the increase, but there is also (especially among the young, and often associated with drug-taking) a great interest in all kinds of occult practices. But that is not all. As in Paul's day, when the trouble was often from the religious people (God's own people, the circumcision at that!) so today, we have plausible preachers who teach all kinds of way-out doctrines, and who are often, as in Paul's day, making a great deal of money into the bargain. There is a devilish lust for something new, something spectacular, not only in signs and wonders but in doctrine as well. In all this we are very much in need of the gift of the discerning of spirits.

As I look back over a fairly long ministry, I feel that if I had my time over again (with the benefit of hindsight of course) I would stop many things which I allowed to continue while thinking to express the Lord's grace and save the person(s) in question, but which I discerned at the time were not of the Holy Spirit. My failure in this caused much of the Lord's work to be spoilt and even sometimes aborted; and the growth which could have happened never developed.

My own experience in the matter of discerning of spirits is entirely different from that of Philip, my co-worker for many years. He is a true 'seer', whereas I do not have this spiritual ability at all. Rather mine has to do with the laying on of hands. I am aware that it is usually taught that it is unwise to lay hands on anyone when demon power is suspected, but Jesus did in the case of the woman with the spirit of infirmity and the following story illustrates the way the Holy Spirit has used me in this connection.

We were invited to take anniversary services in a church in a market town in the Midlands. A local JP was in the chair and everything was very proper and many respectable citizens were at the opening service on Saturday night. After the message—I don't remember what I preached about—I made an altar call and many responded. A fine young man, whom I later learnt was the local youth leader, was one of the first to come to the front. I went to minister to him and, as is my usual practice, I laid hands on him. Immediately I did so, he tumbled from his kneeling position into a heap on the floor squealing like a pig as he went down. That was demon power. That is the way the Spirit allows me to discern spirits. Quickly I commanded the demon to be quiet and to leave, which without more ado it did. After further laying on of hands the young man was quietly and beautifully filled with the Holy Spirit.

This incident naturally caused quite a stir amongst the congregation; and at supper in the chairman's home where we were lodging, I sensed that he was far from pleased at what had happened—as if I could have helped it!—and expressed his view that tomorrow, Sunday, the church would probably be empty as a result. As a matter of fact the church was full to capacity and they were standing outside in the porch and into the street!

Perhaps while dealing with discerning of spirits it will

be wise to add a section on the character and work of evil spirits in general.

A lot of modern theology and psychological theory has eliminated demons altogether, teaching that Jesus was merely speaking in the known language and understanding of his time. This completely denies his own deity, and also the veracity of the gospels, and is therefore totally unacceptable. Further, if one has had any experience of exorcism and seen the condition of people before and after, one is left in no doubt whatever as to the reality and existence of such evil personalities.

The nature of Satan

Satan himself is the arch demon spirit and Scripture paints his character quite vividly and clearly. It would take too long to go into this in any detail but we may mention various characteristics with a Scripture reference in brackets:

The devil is:

1) A murderer and a liar (Jn 8:44);
2) Unclean (Mk 1:23; 5:8 etc.);
3) Seducing (1 Tim 4:1);
4) Frog-like (Rev 16:13–14);
5) Exceedingly fierce (Mt 8:28; Mk 9:18);
6) A seeker of human habitation (Mt 12:44; Lk 11:24);
7) An accuser of the brethren (Rev 12:10);
8) A deceiver—he likes to appear as an angel of light (2 Cor 11:14);
9) He hates to be alone, he prefers to be legion (Mk 5:9);
10) He speaks through men's voices (Lk 4:33; Acts 8:7);
11) He is capable of divination (Acts 16:16).

Sickness caused by demonic power

We have already referred to the woman whom Jesus said Satan had bound and as a result was bent double and could not straighten herself. This was a spirit of infirmity (Lk 13:11).

Luke, the beloved physician, reports that Jesus was 'casting out a devil, and it was dumb. And when the devil was gone out, the dumb spake' (Lk 11:14).

Mark specifically speaks of a dumb spirit in the case of a man who brought his son to Jesus because the spirit not only made the boy dumb but tore his body and caused him to foam at the mouth and gnash his teeth (I have dealt with cases like this); the devil had often tried to destroy the boy by casting him into fire and water. 'Can you help?' asked the man. It was in reply to this question that Jesus answered: 'If thou canst believe, all things are possible to him that believeth' (Mk 9:17–27). When Jesus cast out this spirit he called it a 'deaf and dumb spirit'.

Matthew tells us of another case where a demon had caused someone to be both blind and dumb (Mt 12:22). Another man brought his son to Jesus complaining that his son was 'lunatic and sore vexed'. Jesus rebuked the devil and it departed out of him and the child was cured from that very hour (Mt 17:14–18).

In quite a few of these cases in the gospels it is reported that the disciples had tried to minister healing and failed. This raises two points: (1) If the sickness is due to demon power, then the demon must be cast out and general prayer and anointing with oil will not suffice. (2) Jesus said: 'This kind goeth not out but by prayer and fasting' (Mt 17:21).

Witchcraft, still rife in many third world countries, is demonic. Satan is having some success in bringing this pest into western countries, including our own. I met a case in France where witchcraft had caused the death of a woman's husband and was now attacking her son. The witch in question stood to gain a fortune if he could destroy the son, the last remaining heir.

An English minister now working in Vancouver told me of a case he had to deal with. A demon in a possessed woman spoke through her in a deep man's voice and when challenged as to who he was, he said something to the effect that they were legion, meaning many and that they had recently invaded British Columbia having just come from Africa.

I knew a superintendent minister in the Gold Coast (now Ghana) who told me that witchcraft had closed down three major churches in one town. The witch then joined the missionary's church incognito and under false pretences. Twice he went under cover of darkness to the native pastor's house in order to kill him, but a wall of fire protected the pastor. He returned for a third time one night and an angel withstood him and felled him to the ground. They found him at his home the next morning blind and paralysed. He called for the pastor, who went and prayed for him. As a result he was healed and delivered from his demons and his witchcraft and began to be used effectively in the Lord's service.

It must also be remembered that Satan is a liar from the beginning and tries to insist that there is white magic as well as black magic; and that the white variety is only good and kind and healing. Do not be taken in by such lies. The Bible forbids all occult activity; the Holy Spirit alone is the author of miracles that are glorifying to God.

Finally, a word about the casting out of demons, or exorcism. It is a great fallacy to think that a Christian cannot possibly be vexed with demonic power, just because he or she is a Christian. As Scripture indicates, and as I have learnt from experience, a demon can operate on any of the three levels of human personality —the spirit, soul and body. I have used the word 'vexed' purposely rather than 'possessed'; because it seems to me that a person needs to have committed body, soul and spirit knowingly and willingly to the devil to be actually 'possessed'. The word used in the New Testament means to be 'demonized'—to be as a demon. Not many today in the West go this far, though I have known one or two.

As for a Christian, it seems to me that a demon cannot invade his spirit, which is the location of the 'spirit within' (see chapter two), but he or she can be afflicted in soul or in body. In such cases there is no *moral* content in the vexation. To be vexed in the soul is often the root trouble with people who become extremely depressed or obsessed with fear and anxiety. Psychiatry may help the symptoms, but exorcism is needed for a solution to the problem.

A youngish lady school teacher who was thus afflicted came to see me in a vicarage where I was staying for a week. She described her condition as being conscious of a thick cloud permanently hovering over her head. I commanded the demon to go and immediately she was aware of the cloud lifting and disappearing.

One case above all others stands out in my experience. At a conference in Devon, I and two of my colleagues were warned that a lady who was a devil worship high priestess had agreed to attend for the full week. She had consciously and willingly given herself body, soul and spirit to the devil. The only reason she had agreed to come to the conference was that she had a little daughter whom she dearly loved—the only love of any sort she had ever known in her whole life—and she realized that unless she was delivered from this high-priesthood it would literally be the death of her and leave her daughter alone in this world.

As the conference proceeded she sat in on a few of the meetings for the first few days, but only for a very short time, after which she hurried out. Everybody in the conference was aware of her plight and set about to manifest Christ's love towards her. This was very important. She had never met anything like it before and in the end this was the reason she finally agreed to be prayed for. As the week went on she had stayed longer in the services, heard us praising the Lord and extolling his lordship. She was particularly susceptible to any mention of the blood of Christ and often would go out at that point but generally speaking towards the end of the week she was staying to the end of most of the services.

But one day, unknown to us, she had been in touch with the people of her coven and they had agreed to send evil powers against us as leaders of the conference. The Lord protected us however, so much so that we knew nothing of it all, until the following day when Lady Faith Lees who was caring for her found her bruised and battered in the head and breast. The demons had attacked her when they found they could not get at us!

When we called in her room to see her she at once asked how we were, obviously expecting us to be battered. It was when she found we were unharmed that she told us what she had done, and finally agreed to be prayed for and delivered.

I had been used in exorcism before this conference. Often I had spent long hours and not a few sessions with such cases literally 'wrestling with spiritual hosts of wickedness' (see Eph 6:12), the demon(s) throwing the patient on the floor and tearing him or her (see Mk 9:20). Eventually the name of Jesus and our authority in his name prevailed and the demon(s) had to leave, but both myself and the patient were left utterly exhausted and worn out.

After not a few such cases, I began to think there must be a better way than this. Where is the victory of Christ in such an extended battle? So I sought the Lord and the Holy Spirit took me to two scriptures in particular: Christ 'cast out the spirits *with his word*' (Mt 8:16), and 'Behold, I give unto you power [*exousia*, authority] to tread on serpents and scorpions (no doubt figuratively), and over all the power [*dunamis*, ability] of the enemy' (Luke 10:19).

So, to return to the high-priestess, I opened my heart to my two colleagues and we agreed that in the all-prevailing name of Jesus we would speak the word of authority and deliverance and believe for the confirmation of the word without any wrestling at all. It worked. It was nothing short of a miracle.

12

The Working of Miracles

This gift is often referred to as the gift of miracles; it needs to be noted that the actual gift is the working of miracles. The Greek word for working is *energema* and that is one of the Greek words mentioned in the chapter on the nature of spiritual gifts (chapter four). One definition of this gift calls them 'deeds of power'.

As with demons, many modern theologians have either written off miracles altogether or explained them away. The Reverend James L. Dow M.A. in *Collins Gem Dictionary of the Bible* writes: 'undoubtedly some phenomena described as miracles have a natural explanation. Locusts are wind driven and winds change (Ex 10:13, 19). Quails migrate and need a rest (Ex 16:13). Much that appeared miraculous to the ancients has now been scientifically explained as being perfectly natural, but the miracle is nature itself.'

I am not quite sure just what the Reverend J. Dow means by the final sentence; but surely the miracle is that the locusts and quail arrived at the right place at the right time and such reasoning is applicable to all those miracles that may have natural explanations.

With this in mind it is important to realize that we may expect miracles, small miracles if you will, in our daily life as the Lord's people led by the Spirit of God. These undoubtedly happen in the little everyday happenings of those who have faith for such things. A miracle does not have to be spectacular to be a miracle —it may just be something arranged by God on our behalf at the right place at the right time, which unless God had fixed it would not have happened.

True and exciting as this is, however, it is not really relevant to our present study, because the gift is the *working* of miracles. Miracles, we may therefore adduce, can both just happen and *be made to happen*. It is the latter which manifest the gift.

It is not easy to write satisfactorily about the gift, for three reasons: (1) The gift overlaps very much with the gifts of healing and also the gift of faith—indeed faith is very much involved with the working of all the gifts. (2) Most of the miracles in the Bible are in the Old Testament. (3) There are very few people around these days who manifest this gift, and so we see very few miracles—at least in the unbelieving West.

Let us look at a few of the miracles in the Old Testament. I always think that the most remarkable is where Joshua commands the sun and the moon to stand still so 'the sun stood still in the midst of heaven, and hasted not to go down about a whole day. And there was no day like that before it or after it, that the Lord hearkened unto the voice of a man: for the Lord fought for Israel' (Josh 10:12–14).

I have read that modern science, in connection perhaps with space travel, has found such a discrepancy in the reckonings which can only be accounted for by the truth of Joshua's miracle. Whether that is true or not, I have no means of knowing, but I believe the miracle in any case.

Moses struck the rock, and water gushed out; he also fasted *without water* for forty days (Ex 34:28). To fast without food for forty days is not uncommon, but without water for forty days is impossible save for a miracle.

Israel's crossing on dry land through both the Red Sea and the River Jordan are both miracles, as was also the coming off of Pharaoh's chariot wheels in the middle of the Red Sea.

Elijah being fed by the ravens and his calling down fire from heaven on Mount Carmel are well-known miracles. Elisha, with his double portion, performed many mighty miracles like causing the iron to swim and the widow's cruse of oil to multiply as well as the healing of Naaman from his leprosy.

David's killing of Goliath, Daniel's interpretation of visions and dreams, and the deliverance of the three young Hebrew men from Nebuchadnezzar's burning fiery furnace are all outstanding OT miracles.

Two of the miracles of Jesus other than healing miracles may be cited, because they introduce us into areas where modern miracles have been noted and where we may expect to see them in the future. They refer to food and money.

The feeding of the 5,000 is particularly interesting and challenging because in the first place Jesus said: 'give ye them to eat'. Then, when he actually performed the miracle he did it through the co-operation of the disciples. Jesus divided the five loaves and two fishes amongst the twelve. Little enough for each of them; two fishes between twelve of them—it must have been a bit messy!

Jesus blessed the loaves and fishes and gave them to his disciples and *the disciples gave them to the multitude*

(Mt 14:19). I wonder how much Peter gave to the first person he served? The whole five loaves and two fishes were only enough for a lad's lunch! I also wonder when he had served his first customer how the food multiplied: did the miracle take place immediately after each distribution or immediately before the next one or as the next one was actually being served? I confess I have no idea; also I confess I have never been involved in anything approaching this miracle.

I knew a woman in Halifax years ago who was both very poor and ignorant but who knew the Lord in ways far beyond my experience and who exercised faith for miracles in the depression of the 1930s and would pray for food when the cupboard was literally empty and the Lord replied by sending a food parcel placed on her doorstep. George Müller also believed for miracles of food-provision on a much larger scale, as well as for finance . . . .

Which is the second area for our examination. As a businessman, the Lord's provision of the wherewithal to pay his own and Peter's taxes (see Mt 17:24–27) always had a special appeal to me! Not, of course, that I expect a miracle in the normal course of events to enable me to pay my taxes!

I have known a few minor miracles relating to money though. In the 1970s Loren Cunningham and I were both speakers at a conference in Capel, Surrey. Peter Wallis had just launched out in faith to start a tape ministry but was badly in need of some modern sophisticated machines. It was decided to take up an offering towards this need. As Loren Cunningham waited on the Lord, it was laid on his heart that he should have faith for an offering of £3,000. He brought this to the leaders' meeting and with some misgivings we agreed that he should do this and handle the matter in the service himself.

This he did and asked for a travelling rug to be rigged up at the front of the tent and we should all then deposit our gift into the rug. When the money was all counted up not £3,000 but £11,000 had been given! There had been no sales pressure, just an exercise of faith for a miracle by Loren. I have been involved in two or three similar experiences with money but on a much more modest scale—but with equally miraculous results.

I do not have facts and figures available but I understand on reliable authority that the local finances of not a few churches who have become charismatic have been so increased as a result as to constitute minor miracles. Certainly George Carey's story about St Nicholas' in Durham, *The Church in the Market Place* (Kingsway, 1984) bears testimony to this sort of financial miracle worked through the faith and love of a relatively few saints.

We can rejoice over every miracle, large or small but it still remains a major priority to pray and believe for men and women who will be endued with power from on high to receive this gift and so become *workers of miracles*.

God used a certain Dr Thomas Wyatt, now deceased, to minister faith to my own heart through a most extraordinary ministry and under his preaching two passages came very much alive to me. The first was the story of Joshua commanding the sun to stand still and the second the NT application of this same principle of faith cited by Jesus as follows: 'For verily I say unto you, That whosoever shall say unto this mountain, Be thou removed, and be thou cast into the sea; and shall not doubt in his heart, but shall believe that those things which he saith shall come to pass; *he shall have whatsoever he saith'* (Mk 11:23).

About that time I and two fellow ministers were travelling north from Toronto, Ontario, Canada to take a large funeral in a northern holiday resort by the lake.

It was raining very heavily indeed and looked as though it would continue to do so all day. Joshua's miracle of telling the sun to stand still had made a tremendous impression on my spirit and heart so, as we neared our destination, I mentioned this to my two fellow passengers in the car. They agreed to go along with my suggestion that we command the rain to stop for the time we would be conducting the funeral. This I did in the name of the Lord. As we came out of the church to go to the graveside the rain stopped, the sun even tried to come out. The moment we had finished, the rain set in again for the rest of the day.

In the early 1950s I belonged to a small group of churches in Canada, pastoring one of them. We held a convention in Toronto, Ontario every autumn for our own people, supplying all the ministries ourselves. Then there was a considerable outpouring of the Holy Spirit which transformed most of our pastors including myself. As the autumn approached I suggested we enlarge the basis of our convention, opening it to all God's renewed people and inviting our new-found preaching friends from USA especially Dr Wyatt (mentioned above) from Portland, Oregon.

The Doctor, as we called him, was a mighty man of faith, broadcasting at one time on over 1,000 radio stations every Sunday. It was his preaching under God more than anything else that quickened faith in my life and ministry and virtually changed the whole course of my future life. We advertised the convention on this broader basis and, instead of a few hundred old faces, getting on for two thousand people came to those services; instead of having to struggle to meet expenses of a few hundred dollars the people gave spontaneously between twenty and thirty thousand dollars, the bulk of which we then decided was to be used to send a team to Nigeria led by Dr Wyatt with the renewal message.

The opening services in Lagos were held in the cathedral and were attended by large crowds. A beggar, a complete cripple, who sat begging every day and who was quite a character and well known by the people of Lagos, managed to get into the crowd. As Dr Wyatt was preaching this beggar was so moved that he was edging forward bit by bit on his seat. Dr Wyatt noticed this and at the right moment spoke a word of commanding faith to the beggar and told him in the name of Jesus to walk; which he did. That miracle set Lagos alight and the crowds were very large for the rest of the tour and many churches came into a new dimension of spiritual life as a result of that visit.

This, we may say, is one of the purposes of this gift. It is God's way of advertising. It costs a lot less than man's way—in money that is; how much it costs in spiritual devotion and preparation is another matter!

In Acts 19:11 Luke reports that 'God wrought special miracles by the hands of Paul'. These were apparently in the realm of healing and exorcism. Inasmuch as there are special miracles, it is appropriate that we also expect ordinary ones too, and it is a mistake to expect the special every time.

John's description of Jesus' first miracle when he turned the water into wine is a great favourite of mine and full of inspiration; 'This beginning of miracles did Jesus in Cana of Galilee, and manifested forth his glory . . .' (Jn 2:11). This we may class as an ordinary miracle, set in an everyday occurrence, namely a village wedding; a very important day for the bride and groom, but nothing spiritual or particularly religious about it at all. Yet this manifested forth his glory! We may do the same as 'to another is given the working of miracles'.

Perhaps another warning is not out of place here. Paul reveals that there is to be a revelation of 'that man of sin', the man of lawlessness (RSV) at the time before the second coming of Christ (2 Thess 2:3, 8) and that he will be endued with 'all power and signs and lying wonders' (verse 9). No doubt this is the same man typified by the second beast in Revelation 13 who 'doeth great wonders, so that he maketh fire come down from heaven on the earth in the sight of men . . . And he had power to give life unto the image of the beast, that the image of the beast should both speak, and cause that as many as would not worship the image of the beast should be killed' (Rev 13:13–15).

In the light of all this our Lord's warning needs to be taken very seriously:

> Not every one that saith unto me, Lord, Lord, shall enter into the kingdom of heaven; but he that doeth the will of my Father which is in heaven. Many will say to me in that day, Lord, Lord, have we not prophesied in thy name? and in thy name have cast out devils? and in thy name done many wonderful works? And then will I profess unto them, I never knew you: depart from me, ye that work iniquity (Mt 7:21–23).

But we need not fear to step out in faith, if our hearts are in the right place. A little phrase of mine which has been a source of inspiration in many places is relevant here: 'Remember, it's easy when God does it!'

13
Faith

There are three dimensions of faith. The first two are
fundamental to all Christian life, and the third is the gift
of faith. They are:
1) Saving faith;
2) Faith to live by;
3) The gift of faith (special faith).

We will examine the nature and practice of faith in
general, factors which are basic to all three areas mentioned above; we will then take a passing glance at
saving faith, a more detailed look at a faith to live by,
and take an anticipatory view of the gift.

The nature of faith

Every exercise of faith takes in three areas of the whole
man: namely the heart, the mouth and action, and for
there to be real effective faith, all three areas are synthesized, so that the whole personality is in harmony
and agreed about faith's objective and the means of
attaining that objective. The last sentence encapsulates

all the vital factors relating to faith of any kind and each point is fundamental. Let us examine them in some detail.

The heart

'With the heart man believeth' (Rom 10:10). This is generally accepted, easily said but not so easily practised. So very often when people say that they believe with all their heart (and think they do) in actual fact it is merely a head knowledge that they have. To move from being a nominal Christian to being a real Christian involves faith moving from the head to the heart.

The late Edgar Trout, a great man of faith himself, was going somewhat thin on top and he used humorously to say it was because the Lord had so often to keep patting the top of his head in order to get his faith from his head down into his heart!

Satan knows very well that the one thing that ensures his defeat is a living faith and so he has complicated the subject as much as possible and watered down the whole concept. For instance, in the Bible to 'believe' is 'to have faith', but Satan has brought the verb 'to believe' into ordinary conversational use to such an extent that it has lost its faith content almost entirely. We say, for instance, 'I believe it will rain tomorrow' or 'I believe so and so is right' etc. J. B. Phillips makes the same point very strongly in the preface to his *The Young Church in Action* (Geoffrey Bles, 1955), although he reverses the use of faith and belief to the way I have put it, but he makes the same point. He says:

> These men did not make 'acts of faith', they believed: they did not 'say their prayers', they really prayed. They did not hold conferences on psychosomatic medicine, they simply healed the sick . . . of course the moment one suggests that our tragically divided and tradition-choked church

might learn from this early unsophistication one is accused of over-simplification of the issues involved in our modern world . . . we in the modern church have unquestionably *lost* something whether it is due to the atrophy of the quality which the New Testament calls 'faith', whether it is due to a stifling churchiness, whether it is due to our sinful complacency over the scandal of a divided church, or whatever the cause may be, very little of the modern church could bear comparison with the spiritual drive, the genuine fellowship, and the unconquerable courage of the young church.

The fundamental reason for this loss is just that we have become so intellectualized that our 'intellectualized brain-ridden Christianity', as Tom Smail calls it, has taken the place of the simple naivety of those early disciples who just had hearts filled with a living faith and went out into a hostile world telling what they believed and acting on it to such an extent that 'as a matter of sober historical fact never before has any small body of ordinary people so moved a world that their enemies could say, with tears of rage in their eyes, that these men "have turned the world upside down"' (J. B. Phillips).

So, faith lives in the heart, and not the head. One is not helped when insisting on this, as we must, by the fact that it is virtually impossible satisfactorily to define 'the heart' as it is used in the Scriptures. (So I will not try to do so!) But that it is a much deeper level of personality than the head is obvious.

How then are we to get faith out of the head and into the heart? The answer lies in a simple phrase whose significance is often skipped over: *'faith cometh by hearing,* and hearing by the word of God' (Rom 10:17). It is the 'by hearing' that is the secret. It is so easy to misquote this verse, as it often is, to read: 'faith comes by

the word of God'. People say, 'The Bible says so and
so, the Bible is God's word, therefore it must be true
and so I believe it.' That is a correct statement of fact
but it is not faith.

What then is this 'hearing'? It is when the Holy Spirit
takes the *logos* of God's word and transforms it into the
rhema. These are two Greek words both translated
'word' in the Authorized Version. The *logos* may be
thought of as 'eternal truth', the whole word of God as
revealed in the Scriptures. *Rhema* is the word when it
has become personalized. It is a specific word to a
specific person in a specific situation.

It is the work of the Holy Spirit to transform *logos*
into *rhema*. To do this there must be a hearing, that is, a
hearing by the inner ear of the heart. This is what the
New Testament calls revelation. St Paul prays for the
Ephesians that they may have 'the spirit of wisdom and
revelation in the knowledge of him' (Eph 1:17). Such
revelation is closely linked with 'knowledge of him',
that is, not knowing *about* the Lord, but actually knowing him.

This essential 'hearing' presupposes *meditation* as in
the case of Joshua, a mighty man of faith if ever there
was one. His initial instructions were: 'This book of the
law shall not depart out of thy *mouth*; but thou shalt
meditate therein day and night . . . *then* thou shalt
make thy way prosperous' (Josh 1:8). David knew the
secret, in Psalm 1 he writes of the man of God, 'his delight is in the law of the Lord; and in his law doth he
meditate day and night . . . and whatsoever he doeth
shall prosper' (Ps 1:2–3; see also the many other references to meditation in the Psalms). But we are largely
too busy, often with the Lord's work, to meditate. In
our world it is a lost art. Noise and blaring music have
ousted quiet meditation about anything—especially

God's word.

One's daily 'quiet time' is best used as a time of meditation, rather than a punctilious getting through a set passage of Scripture or even reading the best of notes and commentaries about the passage. The Holy Spirit is the teacher. He, and he alone makes the word of God living and operative as the basis for faith.

But it is not just a matter of a few minutes' daily quiet time; it is a way of life, a letting 'the word of Christ *dwell* in you richly in all wisdom' (Col 3:16). The word of Christ has its home in your heart. Your head, of course understands the word, but then it sinks down deep into the heart, similar to what the popular psychologists teach about getting thoughts into the subconscious, which, they maintain, is very powerful.

A further way of understanding this word in the heart is to remember that Jesus, in the parable of the sower, taught that the seed is the word. In the right soil, i.e. the heart, the seed germinates; it is alive, 'quick and powerful' as Hebrews has it (Heb 4:12). And what happens? It reproduces itself! That is what the Holy Spirit makes possible when he gets the word of God into the good soil of the heart—it reproduces itself. Sow a word of healing into your heart, it will reproduce healing. Similarly, peace, righteousness etc. etc. Blessed word! Living in the heart it creates faith.

Faith is a relationship

When Paul prays for 'the spirit of revelation in the knowledge of him', he again touches a vital aspect of real faith. It is like the relationship of a small child to loving parents. What mummy and daddy say is true, is real, is to be acted on. To question or doubt never occurs to a loving small child, simply because the child *knows* mother and father and therefore trusts them.

In my business days I mixed with a lot of Jewish people. They told a story of a little Hebrew boy who was put on a high wall by his father and told to jump, the father promising to catch him. It was high and he was afraid and argued with his father, but the father promised faithfully he would not let him fall. So the boy jumped and his father did let him fall and he hurt himself. 'Let that teach you a lesson,' said the father, 'never to trust anyone!' Knowing God, and the resulting faith is the exact opposite of that. Underneath indeed are the everlasting arms (Deut 33:27).

Human relationships, especially loving ones, are the basis for much that is fine and noble in life. In love and in business, if the relationship is right, men and women will commit themselves to each other and to activities of apparent risk, just because of the relationship: 'If so and so said so, then I believe it' we say. If that can be true of a human word how much more of the word of the Lord? Do you know the Lord in that way? This is real spiritual growth: 'grow in grace, and in the knowledge of our Lord and Saviour Jesus Christ' says the apostle Peter (2 Pet 3:18). After a lifetime the apostle Paul still cries: 'Oh that I might know him . . .' (see Phil 3:10).

This is the basis for an active living faith, it is not a head knowledge, but in the heart. 'Faith works by love', says Paul to the Galatians and you love with the heart.

The mouth

With the heart man believeth unto righteousness; and with the mouth confession is made unto salvation (Rom 10:10);

We having the same spirit of faith, according as it is written, I believed, and therefore have I spoken; we also believe, and therefore speak (2 Cor 4:13).

You can think all kinds of things, even defamatory things for instance, but you cannot be prosecuted for defamation just for thinking. So long as it is only thinking or believing it is your own secret, no one else knows and you are not committed in any way to it or by it. But once you speak it out, you are committed, everyone now knows, and if it is defamatory you can be prosecuted.

It is this matter of commitment that is the key issue. Once you speak it out you are committed to what you have said, and faith only begins when you are committed to what you believe, especially to what you say you believe.

There is nothing strange about the logic of 2 Corinthians 4:13; it is normal in everyday life to speak out what we believe. 'The train leaves at 9.15 a.m.' a man may say; or 'I am coming to the High Leigh Conference in September' another may say. Two perfectly normal remarks but illustrating the truth regarding speaking what we believe. In the first instance he believes the railway guide; in the second, the brochure intimating that there will be a conference at High Leigh in September. In both cases the only basis for his remark is his faith in what he has heard or read. Because he believes, therefore he speaks and thinks nothing of it.

We read the newspapers, listen to the radio and watch the TV and repeat what we have read, heard and seen. We believe—would to God we would believe what God says as much and as easily as we believe the wretched media!—we believe and therefore speak. Faith is like that. If we really believe, it is no problem to speak.

Romans 10:10 tells us that 'with the mouth confession is made *unto* righteousness'. The speaking of faith is before it happens, because one is sure it *will* happen —that is faith. Anyone can confess afterwards, but a man of faith is so sure of God's word, and his relationship with God and his word, that he can commit himself in speech beforehand. Joshua exemplifies this, he heard from God and so was quite prepared to commit himself to the forthcoming miracle in the ears of all Israel: 'within three days ye shall pass over this Jordan' he said (Josh 1:11).

Action

The third element always present in faith is that which makes the difference between a dead and a living faith. 'What doth it profit, my brethren, though a man say he hath faith, and have not works? can faith save him? . . . But wilt thou know, O vain man, that faith without works is dead?' (Jas 2:14, 20).

This whole paragraph in the epistle of James has been used as a basis for the so-called social gospel, but quite wrongly, in my opinion. Of course we should help feed the hungry and clothe the naked, but that is not the point. What James is doing here is to use illustrations from this area of Christian charity to insist that faith in the heart and on the lips needs to be accompanied by *corresponding action*.

To revert to our former illustrations if we say 'I will see you at the High Leigh Conference', that is an idle and meaningless remark unless I prepare to go to High Leigh and when the day arrives actually set off to travel there.

There is an amusing anecdote that illustrates this point very well. There had been a long hot drought throughout the summer and as a result the crops in a farming locality stood in serious danger and the farmers faced ruin. So the local vicar decided to call a day of prayer and fasting for rain. The farmers duly all turned up at the church to pray for rain. Only one old Christian came with real faith in his heart for the answer to their prayers—he alone brought an umbrella!

The end of this story is that the Lord heard and answered their prayers. When they all emerged from the church it was raining as if a monsoon had arrived. One farmer remarked: 'We prayed for rain, but this is ridiculous!' The general level of our faith is so low and our traditional view of God as being stingy is so ingrained in us that the remark is not far-fetched.

How different was the faith of Elijah (1 Kings 18:41–45). He prayed for rain, not after a dry summer, but after three and a half years of drought. First he actually told Ahab—possibly at the risk of his life—to get up, eat and drink, 'for there is a sound of abundance of rain' before he even went to prayer. That is a confessing with the mouth. Then he went to pray. Six times his servant reported no evidence of rain; then the seventh time, only 'a little cloud out of the sea, like a man's hand'. That was enough. Very soon the clouds were black and there was a great rain.

It is in this area of acting out one's faith that some of the greatest examples of a living faith occur and also some of the greatest tragedies.

In the life stories of two great men of faith, Charles Price of Canada and Paul Yonggi Cho of Korea, both, if I remember rightly, record a miraculous healing of someone in a wheelchair who was so sure that faith would prevail that the wheelchair was despatched home as of no further use before the request for prayer for healing. The person was healed and walked home. Then a second person also in a wheelchair, hearing this, set off and did exactly the same. But in this case there was no real faith in the heart and so the action was not *corresponding action*. There was nothing to correspond to! The whole operation ended in disaster. There was no healing and the wheelchair had to be sent for once again.

I remember being called to the bedside of a man in Denmark who was critically ill with diabetes. He had heard a stirring message about putting one's faith into action and as a result had thrown away his insulin, trusting only the Lord for his healing. It is important to be only loving and understanding in such cases, and not critical of the person who acted in all sincerity and with great courage. I arrived accompanied by Dr Michael Harry (a medical doctor), my co-worker in the work of renewal in Denmark. Michael sized up the situation in minutes and rushed off with a prescription to the local chemist, administered the insulin and saved our brother's life.

Putting these last two essential ingredients of faith—speech and action—together someone has said: 'Faith is an affirmation and an act which bids eternal truth be fact.' That is well put. It underlines too what we have written about *logos*, eternal truth, becoming *rhema*, personal fact. The Holy Spirit works the miracle of faith in the heart first, before both the affirmation and the act.

This leads me to a final, and perhaps the most important, aspect of a living faith. That is: such a faith synthesizes our whole personality, especially of course, the heart, the mouth and the actions, but also the thinking.

The sad fact is that very often one of these parts of the personality is full of faith but is also, usually unconsciously, or perhaps sub-consciously, at civil war with the rest of the personality. A person is very moved by a stirring address on faith and the heart seems just full of the assurance of faith. This is best illustrated by a healing example. After the sermon the heart is sure that the prayer of faith will heal the sick and help is just round the corner. But later, at home, the mind begins to remind the person of the medical fact that the illness is incurable and perhaps also of a similar case known to the person who had the same symptoms and eventually died. A battle begins, a civil war in the personality. Until that is resolved there can be no real faith.

Often I have prayed with folk in the service who have said they had 'all the faith in the world'. At the end of the service shaking hands at the door one automatically enquires of everyone how they are today. In reply the person who had all the faith in the world replies by pouring out the tale of his/her aches and pains and the doctor's diagnosis that it will get worse, or that he/she will have to learn to live with the illness. The mouth and brain are at civil war with the feelings, which have mistakenly been taken to be a living faith.

A wonderful illustration of the positive truth is the case of Peter walking on the water (Mt 14:22–33). When he sees Jesus walking on the water first he is afraid and with the rest of the disciples thinks it to be a ghost. Then when he learns it is Jesus, he remembers that Jesus had constantly been teaching that he wanted his disciples to go out and do the same things that he was doing, that nothing is impossible to those who believe. So, impetuous as ever, he thinks that if the Lord can walk on the water so can he. He cries out to the Lord, 'Lord, if it be thou, bid me come unto thee on the water.' Peter had got the message and I imagine our Lord was very happy about it. In any case immediately he answered with simply one word: 'Come.'

Now let your imagination loose. I wonder what the

rest of the disciples were saying as they saw that Peter intended to go? 'Peter, don't be so foolish . . . use your common sense!' etc. But Peter took no notice. He had heard from the Lord—faith comes by hearing and hearing by the word of the Lord—but I wonder how he set about acting his faith, that is getting out of the boat? All the while his friends were still cautioning him. Do you think he put one foot over the edge and tried the water like we do at the swimming baths to see how cold the water is? Or perhaps he sat on the side of the boat with both legs dangling into the sea? Whatever way, it would take a little time. I wonder what he was thinking? One thing is sure, there had to come a moment when he actually loosed his hold on the boat and committed himself entirely to stand on the water. Did he really expect the water to support his weight? Yes. He was not walking on the water he was walking on Christ's word!

Whichever way he got out—perhaps he took a running jump and leaped over the side?!—it is clear that his whole personality was totally synthesized. If he had stopped to think; if he had listened to the disciples; if he had looked at the waves (as he did later)—in short, if he had believed the evidence of his ears, his eyes, his brain and common sense—he would never have gone. But he had heard from the Lord, his whole personality was in accord that the Lord had called him and he was going. That is faith.

So much for the nature of faith. All these factors in greater or lesser degree apply to all three main areas of faith. Let us take a brief look at these:

Saving faith

This is the well-known message of Luther and the Reformation which took Christianity out of the dimension of the law, depending upon a man's deeds of righteousness, into the realm of accepting the atoning work of Christ at Calvary as being all that was necessary for salvation: 'Even the righteousness of God which is by faith of Jesus Christ unto all and upon all them that believe . . . being justified freely by his grace through the redemption that is in Christ Jesus . . . Therefore we conclude that a man is justified by faith without the deeds of the law' (Rom 3:22–28).

We might pause to notice something that has been a great help and blessing to me personally. Namely that grace and faith are really two sides of the same coin. Quite simply, grace is God giving good gifts to us who do not deserve them. Faith is a means whereby we receive such gifts. So, imagine God in heaven reaching down a hand full of good gifts, that is grace. We for our part, must lift up our hands towards heaven to receive those gifts. That is faith. For every down-stretched hand there is a corresponding upstretched one. Both grace and faith are essential parts of the same operation. They always go together. Grace and faith and the Holy Spirit are always to be found together as also are law, works and carnality.

A well-known hymn, immortalized by Billy Graham, sums up saving faith:

> Just as I am, without one plea,
> but that thy blood was shed for me.
> And that thou bidst me come to thee,
> oh lamb of God, I come.
>
> Just as I am, thou wilt receive,
> wilt welcome, pardon, cleanse, relieve;
> because thy promise I believe,
> oh lamb of God I come.
>
> (Charlotte Elliot)

A faith to live by

A verse that Luther blazoned across Christendom, as everybody knows, was 'The just shall live by faith.' Actually this is still very often a basis for many an evangelical message inviting men and women to come to Christ and become Christians, to be born again; but in actual fact the verse is speaking about living, as distinct from being born, it does not say the just shall be born again by faith, although that is true, what it says is the just shall *live* by faith, and that is a very different thing.

Once one is born again by faith and become a new creation in Christ, one should then begin to live by faith.

The tragedy is that very often, even in the counselling room when first turning to Christ, after the prayer of repentance and acceptance the new Christian is immediately told a series of 'do's' and 'don'ts' which he is expected to fulfil as a Christian. This, I say, is a tragedy, it puts the new-born child squarely on the basis of living under law, yet Scripture teaches that 'Christ is the end of the law for righteousness to every one that believeth' (Rom 10:4).

I was a born-again Christian for half a lifetime, fully dedicated to living a sanctified sacrificial life in the service of the Master, only to find later that I was living under law. I was young and healthy and enjoyed life; I was busy, very busy, and gladly serving the Lord, but never really knowing the joy of the Lord and a free spirit. I was aware of condemnation most of the time, as one must inevitably be when living under law. I was always trying so hard to live up to the standards set by my church, aware that sometimes I failed to do so, and then had to be a hypocrite trying to hide my failure.

These and more are all part of the curse of the law.

Under the preaching of Dr Thomas Wyatt, mentioned earlier, I became aware of a living faith to live by. God convicted me, after days of fasting, that 'without faith it is impossible to please God' (Heb 11:6). I knew I had a *saving* faith of course, but that was years ago. The Holy Spirit then took me to this verse:

> Much more they which receive abundance of grace and of the gift of righteousness shall reign in life by one, Jesus Christ (Rom 5:17).

Much more, *the gift of righteousness* (not struggling and trying ever so hard) and grace—the opposite side of the faith coin—an abundance of grace, lots and lots of it all the time and the same with the gift of righteousness. These are the people that reign in life, that 'live like kings' as J. B. Phillips puts it.

I repented deeply and asked for a little faith to come into my heart, a faith to live by. My whole life and ministry was transformed. I have here only time to give you the bare bones of this experience which took place over many weeks, but it was such a relief not to have to live by trying to be a good Christian.

The gift of faith

The gift, of course embodies all the characteristics already mentioned, only in a higher degree. We may call the gift 'special faith'.

The best way to understand the gift, I think, is to relate what Jesus said in Mark 11. After the incident of cursing the fig tree, which I believe Jesus did solely to lead up to this most important message about faith in the New Testament, he said (translated literally): 'have the faith of God' i.e. have God's faith (Mk 11:22).

When this is granted, that, I believe, is the gift of faith. That is mountain-moving faith. That kind of faith looks at impossibilities and cries 'It shall be done!' Then, as Jesus said, '*he shall have whatsoever he saith*'. Then miracles are only limited by one's vocabulary! Then there is neither the slightest doubt nor a moment's hesitation.

We are all quite happy and familiar with the idea of having the Lord's life, his righteousness, his peace: so why not his faith?

Commanding faith

This view of the gift of faith as distinct from ordinary faith, places its use firmly in the area of what we may call 'commanding faith'. Such faith is to be found in the mouths of the 'heroes of faith' right through the Scriptures. Moses with outstretched hand of authority commanded the Red Sea first to retreat and then to return. Joshua literally commanded the sun and the moon to stand still anticipating Isaiah's prophecy by centuries. God through Isaiah cried: '. . . concerning the work of my hands command ye me' (Is 45:11) though I see modern translations have turned this into a question.

Elijah announced to the evil king Ahab: 'As the Lord God of Israel liveth, before whom I stand, there shall not be dew nor rain these years, but according to my word.' In other words: 'It won't rain until I say so'! And in this connection we need to remember that James reminds us that Elijah himself was a man 'subject to like passions as we are'.

And so we could go on: men of great faith 'subdued kingdoms, wrought righteousness, obtained promises, stopped the mouths of lions, quenched the violence of fire, escaped the edge of the sword, out of weakness were made strong, waxed valiant in fight, turned to flight the armies of the aliens' (Heb 11:33–34).

Others, continues the writer to the Hebrews, 'were tortured, not accepting deliverance' (presumably by compromise), others endured 'cruel mockings and scourgings, yea, moreover of bonds and imprisonment' yet the writer goes on to use these examples of negative faith as a basis to challenge us for whom God has provided 'better things'.

Where, we may ask, are the great men of faith today, who will believe to receive the gift of faith and manifest these 'better things'?

Jesus spoke of a faith that refuses to be gainsaid: 'the kingdom of heaven suffereth violence, and the violent take it by force' (Mt 11:12). What can this mean? The Greek word means 'to be forced'. The kingdom is to be taken by those of urgent vehemence, it is to be seized. Devils are not to be coaxed out but *cast* out. The walls of our Jerichos will fall when we shout with a loud voice and march straight in without fear.

The Syro-Phoenician woman, one of only two to whom our Lord attributed great faith (Mk 7:22–30), had no religious, legal or theological grounds for coming to the Lord on behalf of her daughter, grievously vexed with the devil. Jesus reminded her of her Gentile status and, according to present-day standards, actually rather brutally insulted her, calling her a Gentile dog. But there was a kingdom here that she had glimpsed, an authority of heaven greater than the vexations of the devil and she was not to be put off. Here was violent, vehement urgency and she was for seizing her prize by force. She did. And Jesus commended her.

The other person to whom Jesus attributed great faith was also a Gentile. The centurion who said to Jesus: 'I am a man under authority, having soldiers

under me and I say to this man, Go, and he goeth . . .
Lord, I am not worthy that thou shouldest come under
my roof: *but speak the word only,* and my servant shall
be healed' (Mt 8:8–9, inverted for emphasis).

The word of authority. It is endemic in the gift of
faith.

Jesus spoke the word of command not only to
demons and death but also to the sea and the fig tree.
There was a great storm on the sea, so much so that the
ship was covered with the waves. No wonder even
seasoned fishermen were afraid: 'Lord, save us: we
perish' was their cry. The incredible response of the
master to their cry of fear was this: 'Why are ye fearful,
O ye of little faith?' Mark records Jesus saying: 'How is
it that ye have no faith?' And Luke after the sea had
obeyed the voice of the master reports that Jesus
added: 'Where is *your* faith?' The only implication of
this remark is that Jesus is asking why they had not
done themselves what he had just done for them. 'What
manner of man is this!' (exclamation mark not a question mark) they said wonderingly to each other. What
manner of man? He was a man, the Son of man, speaking not out from his deity, but from his anointed manhood, pioneering a new way for his many brothers to
emulate, acting in the power of the gift of faith.

There is a time and place for prayer—and how much
more do we need both time and place, especially for the
prayer of faith—but there is a time and place also for
the gift of faith, for the word of command in the name
of the Lord who has given us authority over all the
works of Satan.

Peter and John at the gate called Beautiful did not
dither in front of the lame man (Acts 3:1–11). They did
not suggest calling a special prayer meeting, they did
not even pray on the spot. They announced that they

had something! They had the gift of faith and the anointing of the Holy Spirit and they acted and spoke accordingly.

Peter continued throughout his ministry to exercise this gift. He arrived at Lydda where he found Aeneas bedfast and paralysed for eight years. Peter said to him: 'Aeneas, Jesus Christ maketh thee whole: arise, and make thy bed. And he arose immediately' (Acts 9:34).

Not sitting back after this success, he was as a result called immediately to Joppa where he met a very embarrassing and delicate situation. Dorcas had just died and her friends and relatives were naturally very upset and emotional. Peter put them all out. Maybe here is an important lesson for us who are so afraid of offending anybody. First he kneeled and prayed and then he turned to the corpse and *said*: 'Tabitha, arise.' She opened her eyes and sat up (Acts 9:40). Notice that it says Peter turned to the body, squarely facing the problem, not away from it. He still knew he had something!

Likewise Paul, about to be a part of total shipwreck, stood forth and spoke: 'I exhort you to be of good cheer: for there shall be no loss of any man's life among you, but of the ship . . . I believe God, that it shall be even as it was told me' (Acts 27:21–25).

It is recorded that they took notice of the boldness of Peter and John. The members of the sanhedrin marvelled at them. They threatened them and forbade them to speak any more 'in this name'. The response of the apostles and the whole church was to be not in the least concerned about their own safety but rather that they might continue to speak the word with boldness and that signs and wonders would confirm the word (Acts 4:13–31).

Where, again we may ask, are the men of this fearless breed today? Where are those who will believe that Christ has made us co-heirs with himself and bid us go out in his name and continue what he began? It is not in good taste these days to believe and give thanks to God because 'he always causeth us to triumph'. Who we may ask is sufficient for these things? Who indeed? But our sufficiency is of God. The gifts of faith and the working of miracles are still available for men of God who will arise and put their armour on and be strong in the strength which God supplies, through his eternal Son. God's promise is sure, 'Call unto me, and I will answer thee, and show thee great and mighty things, which thou knowest not' (Jer 33:3).

14

Ministry, Ruling and Giving

There are three remaining gifts of the Spirit which are mentioned only in Romans 12. In the AV these are translated ministry, ruling and giving. In modern language to go into the ministry means to become a full-time vicar or denominational minister. Recently in charismatic circles it has also come to mean ministering to people in need through one or other of the gifts of the Spirit like healing or counselling. These are all aspects that have been dealt with in the previous chapters especially the main ministry of a minister, namely preaching; we will not therefore go further into any of this.

In any case what the word ministry means in the Greek is not any of these things, but simply a serving or a ministration.

Ruling also hardly means exactly ruling in any modern use of that word. Some leaders of churches do of course rule to varying degrees, differing from denomination to denomination! But the word 'ruling' conveys the idea of a 'standing before' and is used also in relation to a father's role in a well-ordered home.

Ministry/ruling

So we may put these two gifts of ministry and ruling together in a modern context and say that they cover what is now usually referred to as administration. This ministry, is often (rightly) thought of as the work of *deacons* from the Greek word for ministry.

I have written elsewhere (chapter ten) about the conducting of parochial church council and elders' or deacons' meetings. Suffice it to say here in summary, that to a large extent we have reduced such meetings to the level of normal human committee meetings. But when the first deacons were called they were to be 'men full of faith and of the Holy Spirit'. Stephen was also 'full of faith and power (and) did great wonders and miracles among the people' and Philip went down to the city of Samaria and preached Christ to them and generally had somewhat of a revival there. These were amongst the first deacons.

Now far be it from me to suggest that many of the people on our modern committees are not personally full of faith and the Holy Ghost. That is not meant, neither is that the point. The point is rather that the concept and conduct of these committee meetings were intended by the head of the church to be full of faith and of the Holy Spirit and conducted on that basis, using the available tools for the job. Some people are of the opinion that administration ought to be abolished altogether and that in some vague way we are just to float along being led by the Spirit; but some administration is obviously necessary in a modern world. However we ought to let it be minimal and use the tools for the job.

One further aspect of administration is when it spills over from administration proper and becomes *control*. There is very little scriptural justification for the centralized control that is currently exercised by some headquarters body in many denominations. There are two basic objections to this practice.

1) Speaking the truth in love, (we are to) grow up into him in all things, which is the head, even Christ: from whom the whole body fitly joined together and compacted by that which every joint supplieth, according to the effectual working in the measure of every part, maketh increase of the body unto the edifying of itself in love (Eph 4:15–16).

In this very important passage the emphasis seems to be strongly on 'every joint . . . and the effectual working in the measure of every part'. To revert to the analogy of the human body, as the apostle constantly does, there is only one control-room for each part of the body and that is the head. I see no suggestion in the analogy of the human body, or in the scriptural concept of the church, of one member of the body being in control of other members. The dominant hand has no control over the seeing or the hearing. Each member is in vital contact with the head who controls all in perfect harmony and co-ordination—'from whom the whole body . . . maketh increase of the body'.

2) The whole concept of both the Christian and the church is that we live by faith. A church must be free from control to be able to put its faith into action. For instance, if a local church gets a vision from the Lord, the head, that it should enlarge its borders or spiritualize its worship, if it is tightly controlled from the national or area HQ as to what it can do with its money or how it can conduct its services, then there is little room for faith to be effective.

This is the concept usually referred to in the context of putting new wine into old bottles. Wine is a type of the Holy Spirit and makes glad the heart of man; and new wine is often used as indicating renewal. Jesus said: 'no man putteth new wine into old bottles; else the new wine will burst the bottles, and be spilled, and the bottles shall perish. But new wine must be put into new bottles; and both are preserved' (Lk 5:37–38).

I used to think, as many 'house-church' people still do, that any liturgical form of service was an 'old bottle' that could not contain the new wine. But I have seen liturgy adapted and used delicately and spiritually and become a beautiful framework for divine worship. Undoubtedly, if maintained as a strict unalterable routine with no opportunity for participation by the members of the congregation in the service, then it is difficult to see how the gifts of the Spirit can find a place in such worship. But, I have also noticed that most forms of so called free-church worship can be just as stereotyped and binding.

Money is in many ways central to this matter, because everything in this world costs money, and he who pays the piper calls the tune just as much in church matters as in any other sphere of life.

I was heavily and sadly involved in a situation where men of God in their ministry wanted to move into a new sphere of spiritual life and ministry, their consciences being fully persuaded that God was calling them this way and at peace about it, but because an HQ that held the bag from which their salaries were paid was opposed to this move of the Spirit they were unable to follow the instructions from the head of the church. The headship of Christ had been—and often still is in many quarters—usurped by a council (or executive) of men; honest, sincere, Christian men, servants of the

Lord who genuinely believed that God had called them into this place of control.

The cloud and the fire of God's leading moves on from time to time, and if when the cloud moves men can dictate that we all must stay put, then we are left with a state of *Ichabod*—'the glory has departed'.

This is a delicate matter. There is a ministry of apostleship to guard the church from being 'carried about by every wind of doctrine' and every other 'cunning craftiness of men' and the man of God—or a body of men—will have no trouble in winning the necessary authority to control such things if his/their life and ministry make it obvious that he/they are called of God and endued with power from on high for such a ministry. But such authority has to be won, it is spiritual and not organizational. It was with this in mind no doubt, that Paul wrote to the Corinthians: 'For though ye have ten thousand instructors (school masters) in Christ, yet have ye not many fathers: for in Christ Jesus I have begotten you through the gospel' (1 Cor 4:15).

Giving

Here again we have descended almost wholly to human methods—not even business methods! For if most churches had to produce a business profit and loss account and be accountable to shareholders they would be bankrupt and out of business in no time.

In 1978 I wrote an article for the magazine *Renewal* which the editor at that time Tom Smail entitled 'The Cheerful Discipline and Abundant Reward of Tithing'. That very well sums up a scriptural way of giving, noticing in addition that it speaks of tithes *and* offerings.

The heart of the tithing principle is that God asks through the prophet Malachi, 'Will a man rob God?

Yet ye have robbed me. But ye say, Wherein have we robbed thee? In tithes and offerings' (Mal 3:8). The implication of this language is obvious: you can only rob a person of something that belongs to him. That which is already his own personal property. God regards the tithe as his property. And this is much the best, as well as the scriptural way of regarding one's tithe. It belongs to the Lord; so from the start you never regard it as yours, as part of your income. If you earn £100.00 per week, then £10.00 belongs to the Lord and your usable income is £90.00 and you budget on that. They say what you never had you never miss; and this way of thinking takes any hardship or 'I could never give all that' right out of the question.

The prophet Haggai, who prophesied during an Old Testament time of renewal, without actually using the word 'tithing' asks some very pertinent questions on the subject: 'Is it time for you, O ye, to dwell in your ceiled houses, and this house (i.e. the Lord's house) lie waste? Now therefore thus saith the Lord of hosts; Consider your ways. Ye looked for much, and, lo, it came to little . . . Why? . . . Because of mine house that is waste, and ye run every man unto his own house' (Hag 1:3–4, 9).

This I would think is fair comment on the general church situation in our day—with notable exceptions. The affluence to be seen in most church car parks, the amount of money spent on a night out or a package holiday to Spain or Tenerife, or 'every mod con' in our homes, all contrast devastatingly with the pitiful condition of our church finances.

And talking of contrasts; consider the ease, the majesty and the sufficiency of the simple method of regular tithing as against the hard labour, the puerile indignity and the total inadequacy of sales of work, coffee mornings, raffles and third-rate musical evenings and the like. And think of the spiritual ministry and outreach that could be done in the time given to such money-raising efforts.

As soon as one mentions tithing one is usually immediately confronted with the objection that tithing was an Old Testament system under the law and hence not relevant in our church dispensation of grace. There is some truth in this assertion, but only little. Basically, it is not true. Tithing was instituted not by Moses but by Abraham. To Abraham the tithe was an act of faith, an acknowledgement that God was the source of his wealth; an act of loving recognition that God had, and would supply his needs. 'Know ye therefore', says Paul, 'that they which are of faith, the same are the children of Abraham.'

Nothing is obligatory under the new covenant; therefore we are not under any law that insists we must tithe. You can be a good Christian without tithing; but if it was God's plan for his people's giving under the old covenant, it is surely good—or even 'better'—under the new covenant as the writer to the Hebrews suggests in a rather complicated passage, Hebrews 7:1–6.

With the legal controversy out of the way let us examine tithing as to its principle and practice.

In the Old Testament the whole tribe of Levi were priests and were given no inheritance, which meant they had no personal income; their whole needs were supplied, and well supplied, with everything of the very best from the tithes of the Lord's people. This same principle, Paul insists, is carried forward into the church age. With a veiled touch of humour he says, 'Thou shalt not muzzle the mouth of the ox that treadeth out the corn' (1 Cor 9:9), and argues that, 'Even so hath the Lord ordained that they which preach the gospel should live of the gospel' (1 Cor 9:14). Let the priests enjoy a good table!

Ideally, basically and scripturally the tithe is to be given to the local church where the person regularly worships. The phrase used in the Old Testament is, 'the place which the Lord your God shall choose . . . to put his name there' and there was great insistence that the tithe was to be brought there and not 'in every place that thou seest' (Deut 12:5–14). Some people today, for a variety of reasons, may not want to give their tithe to their local church, or at least not all of it. They point out that in the Old Testament the needs of the stranger, the fatherless and the widow could legitimately be taken care of out of the tithe (Deut 26:12). Hence they argue, possibly rightly, that this is sufficient basis to pay either the whole or part to other sections of the Lord's work, especially to foreign missions, itinerant preachers and more recently to centres of renewal.

Tithing is a healthy discipline which has many things to commend it. It is scriptural. It is an ordered way to express on a regular basis our love for Christ and his church. It adequately and fairly meets the needs of the Lord's servants and the upkeep of the church.

It is a means of opening 'the windows of heaven' for the Lord to pour out such blessings upon his children that they cannot contain (Mal 3:10). British people generally feel that such sentiments ought not to be mentioned, let alone entertained, indeed they even tend to think that to receive anything in return as a result of giving to the Lord is somehow immoral. Nevertheless, British or not, it is written firmly in all the Scriptures on the subject and endorsed finally by our Lord himself when he said: 'Give, and it shall be given unto you; good measure, pressed down, and shaken together, and running over, shall men give into your bosom' (Lk 6:38). St Paul confirms this principle from nature—and how prolific is the harvest in relation to the sowing!—by saying, 'he which soweth bountifully shall reap also bountifully' (2 Cor 9:6). He then adds a great promise which though often spiritualized, was given specifically in relation to money, 'And God is able to make *all grace* abound toward you; that ye, *always* having *all sufficiency* in *all things, may abound* to every good work' (2 Cor 9:8). How stupid to rob God.

Finally we may notice that in times of renewal in the Scriptures, tithing was regularly re-instated and the people responded gladly. In Hezekiah's day, for instance, 'the tithe of all things brought they in abundantly . . . and laid them by heaps' (2 Chron 31:5–6). The priests had enough—and there was plenty left (verse 10).

God is a God of abundant wealth and his nature is to 'give to all men liberally'. We, through grace, have been made partakers of the divine nature, so let us express his givingness by our tithes and his liberality by our offerings.

We have quoted the example from Hezekiah's day in the previous paragraph, now let us look at a modern example. In the April/May 1979 edition of *Renewal* there was an amazing story that illustrated the spiritual method of giving and how it worked in one parish church. It was entitled 'Grace of Giving' and was written by the Reverend Robert Warren who is the vicar of St Thomas' Church, Crookes, Sheffield.

They started to have faith for an initial need in 1972 of £1,250. So the church was called to prayer and sacrificial giving and they decided to have a Gift Day. Although some were very doubtful and others were even sceptical, when the Gift Day arrived the Lord provided

£3,074 as a result of their praying and faith alone.

That was only a beginning. Almost immediately regular giving and giving to missionary work doubled, then doubled again. In six years, despite a £633,000 building project, missionary giving had risen from £1,000 a year to over £10,000 a year.

The tools for the job certainly get the job done if used according to the Scriptures. In five years the *average* giving *per member* of the whole church family had risen to nearly £5.00 per week—and that from people whose average earnings in 1978 were less than £4,000 p.a. All this happened without any pressure and without any continuous mentioning of money but rather all in a spirit of sacrificial giving prompted by the Holy Spirit on the basis of the *worthship* of their God who 'spared not his own Son, but delivered him up for us all', and of their evaluation of their fellowship in the church, members one of another in the body of Christ.

This exercise of faith on a practical monetary level has gone on side by side, one stimulating the other, with an enlargement of the church membership—a 50% increase between 1975 and 1978.

From those initial yet wonderful beginnings, the giving has gone steadily on. One Gift Day in 1976 brought in £7,000 and another in the year after £18,500.

Everything is properly structured and covenanted giving is encouraged, so that in 1979 nearly £20,000 was received back in tax rebates.

This way of giving 'tithes and offerings' is indeed a gift of the Spirit: a very effective 'tool for the job', a very practical one that we may all use and one which puts all of us on exactly the same basis and yet leaves the way open for some with the means to be mightily used in this way. As one great missionary once said: God's work done in God's way will never lack God's supply.'

15
Tools for the Job

The underlying theme of this book has been that the Holy Spirit 'within' and 'upon' and the gifts of the Spirit are the Lord's more than adequate supply of tools to get the job done.

This raises the question: 'What is the job to be done?' The answer, in a word, must surely be to bring in the kingdom of heaven on earth.

This was the constantly recurring theme in the Old Testament prophecies. When John the Baptist began his message it was: 'Repent ye: for the kingdom of heaven is at hand' (Mt 3:2). When Jesus began his preaching it was exactly the same: 'Repent: for the kingdom of heaven is at hand' (Mt 4:17). Of course the kingdom was at hand: the king himself had arrived!

When Jesus taught us to pray he told us firstly to ask: 'thy kingdom come, thy will be done in earth as it is in heaven'. Speaking in relation to his second coming he said: 'this gospel of the kingdom shall be preached in all the world for a witness unto all nations; and then shall the end come' (Mt 24:14). Notice it is the gospel of the 'kingdom', not only the gospel of the saving grace of the Lord. The former includes but exceeds the latter.

The final topic of conversation with his disciples, immediately before his ascension, was 'speaking of the things pertaining to the kingdom of God' (Acts 1:3). It was in this context that he finally introduced the subject of the power of the Spirit resulting from being baptized with the Holy Ghost. The disciples immediately saw the connection: 'Lord, wilt thou at this time restore again the kingdom to Israel?' they asked. They had the right idea, but were thinking of the wrong aspect of the kingdom. 'Never mind that just now', our Lord said in effect, 'But ye shall receive power, after that the Holy Ghost is come upon you: and ye shall be witnesses unto me ('the evidence of me'—see chapter three) . . . unto the uttermost part of the earth' (verse 8).

The message of the kingdom cannot be preached divorced from the power of the Holy Spirit. The one is impossible without the other. They are indivisibly joined as we remember from Mark's gospel 'And they went forth, and preached every where, the Lord working with them, and confirming the word with signs following' (Mk 16:20). That is the gospel of the kingdom.

Paul, looking back over his three years ministry in Ephesus, reports that he had gone about amongst them all 'preaching the kingdom of God' (Acts 20:25); and he finished his life's ministry in chains in Rome still 'preaching the kingdom of God, and teaching those things which concern the Lord Jesus Christ' (Acts 28:31).

How are we to understand the kingdom message? Surely in its simplest form, as our Lord taught: the kingdom of God is *within* the individual Christian and *amongst* his people, the church which is his body (Lk 17:21).

There is also a future aspect of the kingdom related to Christ's second coming when he will come to reign on earth and every knee shall bow and acknowledge him as Lord of lords and King of kings—the kingdom that shall have no end. We cannot consider this aspect here.

The kingdom has no scriptural meaning unrelated to the King. The kingdom has two basic concepts: 1) the authority vested in the King; 2) the state of being King. Both are applicable alike to the Christian and the church.

The whole New Testament message of the Good News was not so much that of forgiveness of sins (though that was included, of course) but that people should 'repent', change their whole way of thinking, outlook and way of life because a new way of life was available—'the Way'—because Jesus was alive, exalted in power and with them in the person and power of the Holy Spirit. The kingdom of God was amongst them; and that was plain to be seen because they were demonstrating it.

Henceforth in Christ a person is 'a brand new person' old things have passed away and one may now reign in life, in all these things more than conquerors. This, I know, is dubbed disparagingly as 'triumphalism' in these days, but it was the Good News of the New Testament, nonetheless; and it is the only message that is ever likely to turn the world upside down. This is already happening in many Third World countries, but that is another story. Sadly, it is not yet our story.

Through the gifts of the Spirit, in their widest connotation, the Lord has made provision for us to express in our lives individually and corporately the authority of the King over Satan and all his works (Lk 10:17–20). Sin shall not have dominion over us. Sickness and disease shall be healed; and demon power exorcized. Circumstances shall not be the determining factor in our life's decisions and behaviour.

Realistically, we see not yet all things under our feet, though the potential is there; but we do see Jesus crowned with glory and honour, not ashamed to call us 'brothers' in the process of God bringing many sons to glory (Heb 2:8–11).

The whole point of Paul's account of Christ's mighty power, when God 'raised him from the dead, and set him at his own right hand in the heavenly places, far above all principality, and power, and might, and dominion, and every name that is named, not only in this world, but also in that which is to come: and hath put all things under his feet' is that God has done all this to give such a Christ as head over all things to the church. That is, to and in and through the church. Christ himself, as the eternal Son of God, *always* had such a position, but *now* he has this position of authority to be *expressed* in heavenly places. It is in heavenly places where we wrestle; where *now* unto the principalities and powers might be made known *by the church* the manifold wisdom of God.

This is the authority vested in the King, which is to be expressed through the church made up of members of the body of Christ who through the abundance of grace and the gift of righteousness are themselves reigning in life.

When this becomes a reality—and there are already indications that things are moving in this direction—it will transform our worship and praise. Worship is elevated into new dimensions whenever people have within the last few days experienced the King exercising his authority on their behalf or through them for the extension of his kingdom in the lives of others. I have found there is no problem to get people freely to praise the Lord in Spirit and in truth when they have *something really relevant and recent* to praise the Lord for. Then it is true, *because of what the Lord has done,* that he is worthy to be praised.

I know that we are exhorted to praise him for what he is, rather than for what he has done. That is right; but the point is that he is a reigning monarch who is active in the lives of his people in his world and not a passive, pious deity in some far off heaven. Further, one cannot help feeling that this pious exhortation is largely an alibi to exonerate one for not having anything to tell of the King's recent activity.

How worship needs a radical face-lift! Very often our time of worship is once a week and it must not exceed one hour's duration—at least not without nasty looks! It is largely routine, uninspired and uninspiring.

The church is run as an organization rather than an organism which is what it is. Its theologians disagree, some are outspoken in denying the faith once delivered to the saints. As a result, the man in the pew—and often in the pulpit!—does not know what if anything, to believe.

The continuous and necessary struggle to raise sufficient money takes up an inordinate amount of time and energy and in the end often results only in an acute shortage of resources.

In short, the man in the street is given a picture of an organization uncertain of itself, its basis and its purpose; struggling to stay in existence and as far as he is concerned, of no contemporary relevance.

By contrast, when we see Christ manifesting his authority over principalities and powers and all the works of the enemy (not only in our theology but in our individual and corporate lives), and see him not only *able to do* exceeding abundantly above all that we ask or think, but also *actually doing* this in our experience, then indeed will there be glory in the church *now*—the 'throughout all ages' bit will take care of itself!

The Lord has ordained that the church shall be a royal priesthood showing forth the virtues of him that has called it out of darkness into marvellous light; delivered it from the powers of darkness, translated it into the kingdom of his dear Son, strengthened it with all might according to his glorious power, and against which the gates of hell shall not prevail.

I think it was Billy Graham who reminded us that in New Testament times the gates of a city were there for the *defence* of the city—and Jesus was speaking of the gates of *hell*—not the defensive gates of the church when he said it was the gates that would not prevail. They will succumb to the church's attack!

Giving his final commission to his disciples Jesus said:

> All power is given unto me in heaven and in earth. Go ye therefore, and teach all nations . . . teaching them to observe all things whatsoever I have commanded you: and, lo, I am with you alway, even unto the end of the world (Mt 28:19–20).

Thus Christ sent them forth with this charter, promising 'I will build my church and the gates of hell shall not prevail against it.' He has given us the tools to get this job done as workers together with him in the partnership of the Holy Spirit.

Church of Jesus Christ: lift up your heads O ye gates; and be ye lifted up, ye everlasting doors; and the King of glory shall come in. Who is this King of glory? The

Lord strong and mighty, the Lord mighty in battle . . .
Who is this King of glory? The Lord of hosts, he is the
King of glory.

Father, let thy kingdom come,
Let it come with living power;
Speak at length the final word,
Usher in the triumph hour.

As it came in days of old,
In the deepest hearts of men,
When thy martyrs died for thee,
Let it come, Oh God again.

Tyrant thrones and idol shrines,
Let them from their place be hurled:
Enter on thy better reign,
Wear the crown of this poor world.

Break, triumphant day of God!
Break at last our hearts to cheer;
Throbbing souls and holy songs,
Wait to hail thy dawning here.

Empires, temples, sceptres, thrones,
May they all for God be one,
And, in every human heart,
Father, let thy kingdom come.

(John Page Hopps)

The Holy Spirit and You

by Dennis and Rita Bennett

The author of *Nine o'clock in the morning* and his wife write on the day-to-day application of a supernatural Christianity. Millions of Christians, both ordained and lay, have received the Holy Spirit as at Pentecost, but relatively few succeed in finding instruction and advice on how to live their lives in the light and power of this experience. This book will answer a real need for many people.

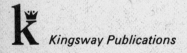

Kingsway Publications